D0320420

CONTRIBUTORS

Text
Michael Munro

Editors
Sheila Ferguson
Mary O'Neill

Consultant Editor
Martin Manser

Publishing Manager
Patrick White

Prepress Controller
Heather Macpherson

Prepress Manager
Clair Simpson

CONTENTS

Introduction

These days, more and more of us are likely to be given the task of writing a report. No matter what sphere of life we are involved in – from the world of business to academic studies, scientific investigation to running a committee – the basic requirements will be the same, as will the skills and techniques needed to achieve a polished, worthwhile result.

You may not have written a report before and may find the prospect a little daunting. This book, however, is intended to guide you through the task by breaking it down into its basics and showing you how to deal with each aspect of report writing, equipping you to tackle the job with confidence. As for those who already have some experience in writing reports, the book will show you how to improve your performance.

It is divided into three parts, each of which will give advice and guidance on tackling one major area of report writing. In Part One we look at the planning that is necessary before you begin, including research and organization of the information that you assemble. Part Two deals with the structure of a typical report, showing you how to construct the framework for your work. In Part Three we look at the process of writing the report, with help and practical advice on such key topics as grammar, style and presentation.

Jargon and technical language are avoided as much as possible, but essential terms are clearly explained in the glossary that follows.

INTRODUCTION

This book can be read from start to finish, but it is also intended to function as a reference tool. It is designed so that you can look up and find specific information that you need as simply and quickly as possible. To this end, many essential items are presented in lists, tables and boxes for ease of reference.

Wherever practicable, the points made are illustrated with sensible and instructive examples, firmly relating the advice offered to the real world of report writing.

Glossary

above in formal writing, this means 'already mentioned'

acronym a word formed from initials or parts of other words. Unlike an abbreviation, an acronym is pronounced as a word

active voice a verb in the active voice is one of those whose subject performs the action of the verb, as in *The dog bit the boy*
▸ see also **passive voice**

appendix (plural **appendices**) an area at the back of a document where material is presented that is too long, complex or distracting to be included in the main body of the text

below in formal writing, this means 'mentioned later'

bold describes type in which the letters are darker and heavier than in normal type, used to highlight or emphasize particular letters or words in a text

bullet point one of several important pieces of information in a list, each introduced by a dot or other symbol

buzz word a fashionable word, especially in the jargon of a particular profession or group, used to give the impression of being 'in the know' and up to date

cardinal number a number that indicates quantity, eg *one, two, three, 99*

cartridge the container for ink in a printer

clause a sequence of words that includes a verb

colloquial used in everyday conversation and informal writing rather than in formal writing

GLOSSARY

common noun any noun that is not a proper noun, eg *table*, *book*
▸ see also **proper noun**

comparative the form of an adjective or adverb used to compare, saying that someone or something has more or less of a quality than someone or something else, or than before

consonant any letter that is not a vowel; a speech sound made by blocking the passage of the breath in some way

desktop publishing the facility to carry out typesetting, design, layout, illustration, etc of a document or publication on a desktop computer

direct speech speech reported in the actual words used by the speaker
▸ see also **reported speech**

font a complete assortment of typefaces for one sort of letter

house style the set of rules about use of language and presentation of text adopted by a particular organization

idiom an expression with a meaning that cannot be understood from the usual meanings of the words that form it, as in *have a finger in every pie*

idiomatic (of expressions) typical of a native speaker of a language

indented this describes a line (or lines) of text beginning not at the left edge of the main text but slightly to the right of it (just like this line!)

infinitive the base form of a verb, from which other forms are made

irregular (of a verb or plural form of a noun) not formed in the standard way

italic describes type in the form of sloping letters, used to highlight or emphasize particular letters or words in a text

lower case (of letters in type) small, as opposed to capitals or upper case
▸ see also **upper case**

metaphor the use of an expression to describe something that it does not literally apply to, as in *He was a lion in battle*

ordinal number a number that indicates a position in a series, eg *first, second, third, 31st*

parenthesis where material is placed that is not vital to the text but contributes to it in some way, indicated by brackets or commas

passive voice a verb in the passive voice is one whose subject is the person or thing that an action is done to, as in *The boy <u>was bitten</u> by the dog*
▸ see also **active voice**

person the form of a verb as it relates to who or what is speaking (**first person**), spoken to (**second person**), or spoken about (**third person**)

phrase a set of words that expresses a single idea and forms part of a sentence

political correctness the avoidance of expressions that may be understood to exclude or denigrate some people

predictive spelling the facility of some spellchecks (and indeed of text messaging programs) to predict what you are likely to mean and fill in the rest of a word when you type only the beginning of it

proofreading the careful reading of printed pages to look for mistakes in spelling, grammar, etc

proofs printed pages of a text that are used for careful reading and correcting before the final version is printed

proper noun a name given to a particular person, place or thing, typically starting with a capital letter, eg *Barcelona, Alice*

GLOSSARY

questionnaire a prepared set of written questions used to gather information or compile statistical data

register the form of language used in particular circumstances or when dealing with particular subjects, such as formal or informal, technical or general, etc

regular (of a verb or plural form of a noun) formed in the standard way

reported speech a person's words reported with the necessary adjustments of person and time, as in *He said he was leaving*
▸ see also **direct speech**

roman describes type that is in the standard form, not italic or bold

running title the title of a book, article, etc printed repeatedly at the top of each page

simile an expression involving a comparison between two things, as in *The effect of the news was like a thunderbolt*

suffix one or more letters added to the end of a word to create a new word, eg dark<u>ness</u>, owner<u>ship</u>, end<u>less</u>

superlative the form of an adjective or adverb used for saying that someone or something has the most or the least of a quality than anyone or anything else

synonym a word that has the same (or nearly the same) meaning as another word

thesaurus a type of reference book containing lists of synonyms (or near-synonyms) of a word that you want to replace in a piece of writing. Some word-processing programs also offer a thesaurus facility

upper case (of letters in type) large, or capital, as opposed to lower case
▸ see also **lower case**

voice see **active voice, passive voice**

vowel any of the letters *a, e, i, o* or *u* (and sometimes *y*) that represent a speech sound made with the mouth open and the passage of the breath not blocked in any way

word processor a machine (or a software program) that enables you to type, arrange and store text electronically

Part One
Planning your Report

What is a report?

This may seem like a silly question, but when you are writing a report, or indeed creating any piece of written work to be read by people other than yourself, it is important to be clear about exactly what it is you are trying to do. Let's look at a dictionary definition.

> **report** *n* a statement of facts; a formal or official statement, such as of results of an investigation or matter referred ... ...
> *The Chambers Dictionary*

The words 'facts' and 'results of an investigation' are key terms here, which will come up again as we look at the task. Generally speaking, a report is a document that is meant to contain material that will be of use and interest to those reading it. It may be intended for the eyes of only a few people, for example the writer's immediate superiors within a company or other organization, or it may be for wider publication, such as in a trade journal or a consumer publication like *Which?*. Irrespective of its target readership, its sole purpose is to give information, not to amuse people or show off your writing skills.

This is not to say that a report must be a dry and dull piece of work that cannot be enjoyable to read, but rather that the focus must always be on presenting information as clearly as possible. With a possible few exceptions, such as a feasibility study, a report by its very nature will deal with something that has gone on in the past, whether recently or some time ago, and is therefore based on facts that can be put together and demonstrated, not mere speculation or an account of your own opinions.

Whether it is a single page or several hundred pages long, a good report needs to be well researched, carefully planned, clearly laid out and written in a fluid and persuasive style.

There are, of course, many different types of report, with several essential features in common as well as their own particular fields of specialization. For example, here is a list of some of the most frequently commissioned types:

- annual report
- case study report
- committee report
- comparative advantage report
- cost-benefit analysis report
- feasibility study report
- field study report
- financial report
- health and safety report
- inquiry report
- laboratory or experiment report
- minutes
- progress report
- quality monitoring report
- research report
- technical report

You may be familiar with some or all of these. Depending on your own field, the report you are interested in writing may well be among them. Let's look at these examples in detail.

Annual report

An annual report is typically one produced by a business or other kind of organization for presentation to those who attend its AGM (Annual General Meeting). It will include various sections, some of which will take the form of reports themselves. For example, it will probably feature a *Chairperson's Report* on the main activities that the organization has been involved in during the year since the last AGM, perhaps congratulating the achievements of particular departments or individuals. It is also likely to contain a *Treasurer's Report* covering the finances of the organization, detailing income and expenditure over the past year, assets and liabilities, and ending with a balance sheet. It may also be distributed by mail to those who are unable to attend the meeting itself.

Case study report

A case study report is an account of an event, subject of investigation or inquiry, activity, etc that gathers and organizes information based on analysis of one or more cases or case histories. The case (or cases) involved may be an example of those handled by any of a range of professionals, including social workers, engineers, and medical practitioners. The point is that it relates to concrete instances and the study of these. It is used to point up valuable lessons that may be learned from involvement with the complexities of real-life situations, as opposed to the purely theoretical or hypothetical, and how these lessons could be applied in future.

Committee report

In organizations of any size, work will tend to be divided amongst committees, groups of people who are assigned particular tasks or areas of activity. Their accounts of how they have tackled their assignment or ongoing work over a period of time will make up the bulk of the report that they will be obliged to submit to their superiors or the organization as a whole. The writing of such a report may be delegated to particular committee members, perhaps holding official titles such as Chairperson or Secretary or it may be the responsibility of the group as a whole.

Comparative advantage report

Comparative advantage is a business principle which states that an individual company or country will perform better in a particular field of economic activity than another company or country. For example, one country may be able to produce goods more cheaply because of having an abundant and low-paid workforce, or a business firm may be able to sell its products at a higher price than its competitors because of a reputation for quality and excellence. This kind of report looks at different producers and different areas of business, gathering and analysing data to help identify areas where comparative advantage might be found and exploited.

Cost-benefit analysis report

Cost-benefit analysis is essentially the comparison of the resources used in a particular course of action with the benefits to be derived from it. A report on this will be used to decide whether or not an activity will be profitable or otherwise worth doing. For example, a company may be considering the introduction of a new IT system. A cost-benefit analysis report will be expected to look at such areas as: the functioning of the present IT system and what problems it may have; whether or not a new system would address these problems; assessing the proposed new system for cost, efficiency and reliability; identifying the means of monitoring the new system and collecting the relevant data. The findings of such a report will play a vital part in the decisions on future activities of those commissioning it.

Feasibility study report

A feasibility study is an investigation into whether or not a particular project, system, line of product, etc is practicable or desirable, and also financially viable. A report on such a study will look at the proposed new systems and processes, the objectives of these, the sources of information available, the financial implications and any problems or issues arising from them. It will compare different alternatives in terms of constraints and limitations, necessary developments, implementation issues, costs and benefits, risk factors, efficiency, impact on the organization in terms of staff, training, etc. It will conclude by making recommendations as to which alternative is most desirable and whether or not it should be adopted.

Field study report

A field study is essentially a research project carried out on an activity performed in practice, in everyday life as opposed to in a classroom or laboratory or in theory only. For example, a restaurant opening in a new location may commission a field study into the effectiveness of its advertising leaflets. The study might involve door-to-door interviews with members of the public to whom leaflets were delivered, telephone surveys, questionnaires given to customers asking (among other things) whether or not they heard about the restaurant through leafleting. The report would collate and analyse all such data and present its findings, allowing the restaurant owners to decide whether or not leafleting was an effective form of advertising.

Financial report

A financial report looks at the position of the finances of an organization, whether it is a literary society or the government of the United Kingdom. It will cover all income and expenses for a given period of time (such as a financial year), administration costs, salaries paid, investments made, grants or awards, tax payments made, etc. It will usually assess assets held both at the start and end of the period and list any liabilities which remain unpaid. A financial report is particularly important in providing information on the viability of the organization and its findings will be used in preparing annual budgets.

Health and safety report

This kind of report covers issues of health and safety in an organization, whether annually or at more frequent intervals. It will contain information on such matters as accidents and injuries in a workplace, the provision of First Aid, safety audits, risk assessment of new premises and equipment, the use of dangerous materials and the presence of hazardous substances such as asbestos in buildings, fire regulation and drills, and the appointment of health and safety officers or committees. It will usually indicate the level of compliance of the organization in terms of basic health and safety criteria and make recommendations for improvements.

Inquiry report

An inquiry is an investigation into something, such as an accident or other incident or an ongoing problem. Its purpose is to identify the causes of the incident or problem and recommend action to remedy the problem or prevent further similar incidents. The inquiry report will publish the findings of those conducting the inquiry. It should cover such matters as:

- identifying the purpose of the inquiry and those who are to undertake it
- the methods to be used
- details of the nature of the problem or the events involved up to and during the incident
- any action that has already been taken in response
- recommended remedial or preventative action

Laboratory or experiment report

This kind of report is highly empirical, that is, it is very much concerned with experiment or trial. For that reason, it will tend to concentrate on such matters as the hypothesis that is to be tested, assumptions made, materials and methods (complete with detailed sizes, quantities, concentrations, timings, etc), precise details of any equipment used, and any statistical methods used to analyse the data that is gathered.

As well as a glossary, it may often be necessary in this type of report to include a list of symbols that are used in the text.

Results may often be recorded on special forms or logbooks designed for the purpose and as they are concerning scientific data, it is vital that they are recorded immediately and accurately. Much use will usually be made of graphs, tables and charts.

The section on results will be important, particularly in terms of their analysis and evaluation. The soundness of the conclusions will be discussed, including any anomalous results (and reasons for accepting or rejecting them), possible alternative interpretations of the results, and the extent to which the results may contribute towards an understanding of the broader topic of study. Recommendations may be made for further experiments or improved methodology in further testing of the hypothesis.

Minutes

Minutes are a special kind of report, the subject being a formal written record of a meeting, whether of committee members, a sales force, a club or members of a trade union. They summarize what happened and who said what, including any disagreements and complaints. Minutes are usually written in the past tense, using simple impersonal language, with reported speech used rather than direct speech.

Minutes need to be concise. They should present only the essential parts and dispense with any unnecessary details. It is best to write them in short sentences and short paragraphs. They also need to be accurate, neutral, clear and complete, so that anyone who did not attend the meeting can follow the discussions that took place and understand how and why decisions were made, and also so that those who were present find nothing in them to disagree with.

Minutes follow a standard format, which usually includes:

- a heading that states the type of meeting or its purpose, the name of the organization or group holding the meeting, and the date, time and venue
- a record of who was present and a note of any apologies for absence
- a record of corrections to the minutes of the previous meeting, if there are any, together with a statement that the previous minutes were read and approved
- a summary of what happened at the meeting, including correspondence that was received, opinions that were expressed, decisions that were made and summaries of reports that were presented (such as the Chairperson's Report or the Treasurer's Report)

- if required, 'action points' can be added to record who made decisions about steps that have been agreed, who is responsible for carrying these out and when they need to be completed
- any other business: a call for those present at the meeting to bring up any other matters suitable for discussion
- the date, time and venue of the next meeting

Each individual point made in the minutes needs to be numbered so that it can be easily referred to at the next meeting. If a numbered section includes several points, these should each be numbered in the style *2.0*, *2.1*, *2.2*, etc.

For obvious reasons, minutes should be based on notes made during the meeting and written as soon as possible after the end of the meeting. Copies should be sent to those who were present, and to those who should have attended but were unable to do so. The minutes can then be read through by everyone and, hopefully, approved without any objections at the next meeting.

You can see an example of a typical minutes document on page 12.

Scott-Fourneaux Group
Senior Management Team

Minutes of meeting held at group headquarters on 7 July 2006, at 3.00pm
Present: Joanna McGarrigle (Chair), Marie Eagelton, Bob Newman,
Ana Maria Tejos, Steve Vandersteen, Diane Moore, Richard Mills,
Denis O'Leary

1. Apologies
Apologies were received from Jill Thornton and Will Pidgeon.

2. Minutes of previous meeting
The minutes of the meeting held on 16 June were approved and were accepted as a
true record.

3. Matters arising
BN reported that the business graduates have been notified about the date of the
project presentations.

DM thanked the Human Resources Department for their reports, all of which have
been received.

Still awaiting confirmation of the Wright Rooms for September seminars.

4. Reports
The reports were distributed. SV suggested that each should be summarized. The
chair stated that in view of the absence of JT and WP, this should not be done at the
meeting. Following discussion it was decided that this could be done informally outside
the meeting if anyone needed information that was not included in the reports.

5. Action points
Half-year sales figures to be collated by ME and AMT for presentation at the next
meeting.

DO to make travel and accommodation arrangements for CEO's visit to Paris
suboffice in November.

6. Any other business
RM asked about progress on sourcing new office printers. The chair stated that
research was ongoing and a report was expected by the end of the month.

7. Date of next meeting
Same venue, 8 August, at 11.00am.

Progress report

A progress report is written to inform an employer, manager, associate or customer about progress that has been made on a project during a given period of time. Obviously, this kind of report is only relevant when a project is expected to be reasonably long-term, and will be made at an agreed point on a schedule. It will include information on such topics as:

- how work is going in general (smoothly/quickly/slowly, etc)
- how much has been done
- what is currently being done
- what remains to be done
- any problems that have arisen (and how they are being dealt with) or are anticipated
- whether or not the target date for finishing the work is likely to be met
- whether or not the budget is being adhered to

The essential function of this report is to demonstrate that progress is indeed being made, as well as to keep those who need to know up to date, but it will also give those who read it the opportunity to assess the work to date and perhaps indicate desirable changes.

Quality monitoring report

This kind of report is concerned with the maintenance of a standard and is accordingly carried out at regular intervals. The quality involved may relate to such things as the purity of air or drinking water, the effectiveness of teaching at a school or university, or whether or not a manufactured product continues to meet predetermined standards.

Such a report will make clear who is responsible for the monitoring process and what its scope is, as well as setting out its methodology (means of assessing quality, how information is gathered, standards to be met, etc). Problems or failings will be identified and different kinds of remedial action necessary to maintain quality will be discussed, resulting in appropriate suggestions. One of the by-products of such a process will usually be the identification of 'best practice' and recommendations for its wider application.

Research report

Primarily, a research report is a permanent record of research that has been done, often the only such record. Those who read it may be interested in the specific area studied; they may simply wish to keep abreast of current developments in the field; they may be looking for relevance to their own, related discipline. There are many different areas of research, from market research to medical research, but reports in each field will tend to follow a similar pattern. They will generally include the following:

- a description of the purposes of the research, and its most important element(s)
- a list of those who carried out the work
- a description of how this research relates to existing research
- exposition of the results, including how they were reached and verified
- estimation of the consequences for the topic in question
- if the research is to be published, a statement of where it might be expected to appear

Technical report

By its very nature a technical report is totally factual and intended to be read by professionals rather than a lay audience. It will focus on a highly specific topic and aim to supply its readers with detailed information on that subject, whether it is the operation of a new model of car engine, global warming, characteristics of a new form of medication, or the recycling of newsprint. Because of this it is more likely to contain lots of statistics, tables and graphs rather than being a flowing work of literature. It may study a problem and examine the feasibility of various solutions; it may evaluate a project and make recommendations.

A common form of technical report will look at a new product design and assess it in terms of intended function, its construction, the materials used and its special features, compare it with the competition and decide whether or not it is marketable. Whatever its subject, its findings will be highly practicable.

The types of report detailed above represent some of the most common varieties but the list is by no means exhaustive. It may well be that the report you need to write has not been covered: don't worry. What we have to say in this book is meant to be applicable to any type of report.

Clarifying the task

Now that we have settled the matter of what a report is, we can start to look at the processes involved in actually writing one. To clarify the task in your own mind before you begin, you might find it helpful to give some thought to the following questions:

- Who is this report for?
- What exactly do they want to know?
- What style of report do they want: formal or informal? fancy presentation or just plain facts and figures?
- What will they use the information for?
- What is the target date for completing the report?
- How long should it be?
- Is there a limited budget for the production of the report?

If you don't have the answers to these questions, you should make an effort to find them out before going any further. What you learn will equip you to tailor your report to its audience. Otherwise you may produce a piece of work that you are perfectly satisfied with but which fails to fulfil the purpose that it was intended for. To show how important this is, it would be a good idea to look at an example.

Let's say you have been given the task of producing a report on the results of the trials of three different makes of computer printer. If the report has been requested by, say, a purchasing department in a car dealership with the idea of finding the best printer for internal stock lists, they will probably want to concentrate on issues of economy. They will be looking to identify the printer that will do an acceptable job for the best price; they will want clearly presented facts and plenty of statistics produced as hard evidence.

On the other hand, if the report is being commissioned for a PR department in an advertising firm they are likely to be more interested in a high-quality result in the finished, printed documents and will be less concerned with cheapness. They may very well request printed samples to be included. They may even be looking for an element of aesthetic judgement from the report writer.

As for length, you may be given a minimum or maximum extent, but if not, a good rule of thumb is to err on the side of being concise (while still being sure to cover all essential points) rather than risk boring your readers by being excessively long-winded or discursive. Length is easy to monitor using your PC's word-count facility. If not working on computer, however, the best way to keep a regular check on the number of words you are writing is as follows. Take what looks like a typical stretch of writing and count off ten lines of it. Count the number of words in these ten lines, then divide that number by ten. This will give you the average number of words per line. If you then multiply this by the number of lines on a page this tells you the average number of words per page. From then on you can assume each page will contain this number of words.

Is there a limited budget for the production of your report? Some reports, especially the more complicated or extensive ones, will inevitably involve expense. For example, certain parts of your research, such as questionnaires or surveys, may well have to be paid for. Perhaps such costs will come out of your own pocket, to be reimbursed later when you claim for expenses; perhaps you will be allotted a specific sum in advance. The actual reproduction and printing of the finished report may also be an expense that will have to be taken into consideration.

Of course, this may not be relevant if your report is to be brief or an in-house document only, but if budgetary limitations apply to your report it is up to you to make sure that you don't go over budget. It will be a pretty poor reflection on your work if you are unable to deliver the commissioned report because you have run out of money or if you have to apply for additional funds in order to complete it.

While the emphasis and procedure may be different for each of the two reports mentioned in the example above, in each case the information will be used for the same essential purpose: to allow those for whom it is written to make an important decision by presenting them with all the information that they need.

Drawing up a plan

It is always a mistake to start writing without a clear plan in mind to guide you, step by necessary step, to the finished result. Without this, the risk is that you will end up with something that is incoherent, full of digressions, repetitive and therefore utterly useless for its purpose.

At the same time, it is important not to begin with too many assumptions about what you are likely to find. Try to be objective and keep an open mind. There is no point in setting out to bend the evidence to bear out whatever bias you begin with.

Be patient in your preparation, and don't be tempted to take shortcuts. It is perfectly understandable to be keen to begin and get the job done as quickly as possible, but, as with many tasks, time set aside for thorough preparation is not time wasted but time well spent. There is nothing more frustrating than having to scrap something you've worked hard on simply because you have been going in a wrong direction or have run across something you ought to have included but didn't make provision for. Thorough groundwork will provide the foundation on which your report will be built and there is no easy substitute for this.

Don't get carried away, however! It is important not to lose sight of the date by which you are expected to produce your report. Above all, don't be late. If your report is intended to influence or convince other people they may just become prejudiced against it simply through being kept waiting.

The following are suggested stages into which you can divide the preparatory work before putting pen to paper or finger to keyboard:

- Ask yourself questions.
- Try mind-mapping.
- Carry out any necessary research.
- Gather all available information on the subject.
- Choose the information that is most relevant for your purpose.
- Organize your information into a well-defined structure.

Ask yourself questions

Particularly if you have absolutely no idea of where to start, it may help to begin by asking yourself the questions *why? how? who? what? when? where?*. Dealing with these simple and straightforward queries is guaranteed to at least get you thinking constructively about your task. For example:

> *Why is this report being commissioned?*
> *How is it to be done?*
> *Who is commissioning it and who is going to want to read it?*
> *What is it supposed to be about?*
> *When is it expected to be completed?*
> *Where is it to be delivered?*

OR

> *What happened?*
> *Who was involved?*
> *Where did it happen?*
> *When did it happen?*
> *How did it happen?*
> *Why did it happen?*

Try to imagine the kinds of questions that your reader might want to ask you if they had the chance to speak to you in person, and you won't go far wrong.

Mind-mapping

Perhaps you have never written a report before, and you find yourself at a total loss as to how to begin. The blank computer screen or sheet of paper can be daunting even for an experienced writer. The point is to get started, get something down in words, even if you find it has to be discarded later. 'A journey of a thousand miles begins with a single step', as the Chinese philosopher Lao-tzu once said.

Mind-mapping can be a fruitful way to get going. It may sound like some kind of scary psychological procedure, but it is really only a preliminary technique for allowing your ideas to flow, like a sort of single-handed brainstorming. Essentially, all you have to do is create a kind of map or chart of ideas. Take a large sheet of paper and draw a box in its centre. Write the subject of your report in this box. Think about things that might be relevant to this subject and write them somewhere on the sheet (it doesn't matter where) and draw a line connecting each one to the central box. You will probably find that one thought leads immediately to another; write them all down, even if they seem unlikely or flippant. It is important not to be hampered by preconceptions: this is an opportunity to consider all aspects however outlandish they may initially appear.

In this way you will get down on paper all of the various ideas that seem relevant but are not obviously connected. Once you can see them in black and white you can begin to draw lines joining them with one another as well as with the main topic. As other aspects occur to you, it is easy to write them in and link them with what is already there. Before you know it, you may well have generated a rough structure for your report.

Essentially, research in report writing simply means seeking out the information that you are going to need to begin writing knowledgeably about your subject. In many cases it is easier to begin with personal contacts. It may be that you know of specific people who can answer questions for you, particularly within your own organization or company, or whose work in the field is relevant and readily available to you. Perhaps you work for a company with an extensive database that you can use as a primary source.

Outside your own organization, there may be bodies which you can approach, such as trade or professional associations, many of which may publish regular journals or reports of their own. For example, *Which?* (formerly the Consumers' Association) reviews and tests thousands of products every year, from cars and computers to holidays. The kind of information that such bodies routinely gather may be just what you need, and this will save you a lot of spadework. Try not to reinvent the wheel!

Interviews and meetings

You may want to interview specific people or even organize a meeting to bring several individuals together for a discussion of the topic of your report. If this is what you want to do, bear in mind the following points:

- **Be courteous**; people will be more inclined to help if asked nicely.

- **Be flexible**; other people's time is as valuable, if not more so, than yours, so go out of your way to accommodate their schedules rather than impose yours on them.
- **Be clear about what you want to achieve**, and make sure that the others involved are fully informed about your goals.
- **Be consistent in obtaining your information**; the value of your research will be that much less if you fail to ask everyone the same questions.
- **Be methodical in recording the information you obtain**; take notes during the interviews or meeting rather than trying to remember what was said later.

Surveys and questionnaires

Information can be gathered in a wider and more anonymous way by the use of surveys and questionnaires, whether on paper or carried out by e-mail. A well-constructed questionnaire, asking all the right questions and allowing people simply to tick boxes, without having to give their names, has the advantage of collecting information in a standardized way, making it easier to compare and consolidate the results. This method also means that there will be no personal bias in your mind (whether conscious or unconscious) as to the value of individual opinions because you will not be aware of who has said what. Here are some guidelines for creating a useful questionnaire:

- Keep your language simple and clear: sometimes people will see your questionnaire as a chore and will be only too ready to put it aside. Make it easy for them: people can't answer a question if they can't understand it.
- Keep each question separate, requiring a separate answer; double questions will only confuse people.
- Keep your questions short and to the point; people will tend to lose interest or fail to grasp the real issue with long-winded or complex questions.

- Use what are known as 'closed questions', that is, ones that should be answerable with a simple 'yes' or 'no'; collating your findings will be easier to manage. (There may be some areas however where an 'open question' is required, for example you may wish to ask the respondents for their opinions or recommendations.)
- Don't ask leading questions, such as 'Do you agree that Printer model A is by far the best?' Many people will be swayed by this kind of question to unthinkingly agree with the suggestion, thus giving you inaccurate and biased results.
- Use a simple and clear layout so that people can immediately see what it is they are expected to do.

Libraries

Libraries have always been good places to begin researching, with their stocks of regularly updated reference books, such as *Whitaker's Almanac*, *The Statesman's Yearbook*, *Who's Who* or the *Dictionary of National Biography*. You may not be familiar with these titles, but on your next visit to a library it might be a good idea to take one or two of them down from the shelves (they tend to be kept for consulting in the library only, not for borrowing to take home) and have a look at what they contain. You might immediately see relevant material.

Whitaker's Almanac, for example, has been published annually since 1869 and contains detailed statistical information about the year ahead, including astronomical data and charts of the tides. In it you will also find detailed statistics about the government, public bodies and current events.

When you are looking for factual information, encyclopedias will offer you just that, and on a wide range of subjects. The largest and most comprehensive, such as the *Encyclopedia Britannica*, run to many hefty volumes, but there is a range of single-volume encyclopedias that may well provide you with what you want to know. You might need to be a little careful when looking up information about subjects such as politics in an older encyclopedia, as this sort of information can quickly become out of date. Always consult the most recent encyclopedia you can find, and, if you are in any doubt about its being up to date, think about confirming what it says in another source.

A good library's non-fiction section will be helpfully divided into different topics and fields. Try browsing there for what you need. If you don't find exactly what you are looking for, you can make a request for specific books to be sent from another library. (This may involve a fee.)

Many libraries also hold archives of newspapers, magazines and other more specialist periodicals, whether as physical copies or on microfiche. Libraries will also usually have photocopying facilities, which means you won't have to borrow books or periodicals but can simply photocopy the relevant material once you have identified it. Increasingly, those without a computer of their own can also head for their local library for Internet access. An Internet café is another place where you can go on line for a fee.

The Internet

The Internet, of course, contains an amazing array of information, and the use of search engines such as Google, Yahoo, AltaVista, AskJeeves and Lycos allows you to quickly track down the topics you are interested in. The Internet is especially useful if you are looking for the most up-to-date information that is available. You are more likely to find current information on line than in a reference book that may have been printed a year or more ago.

However, while the Internet is a highly useful and speedy tool it is one that must be used with caution. Material that you find on academic or governmental websites can usually be relied on, but the content of many Internet sites is not checked independently and you should not accept all you find at face value. Be aware that the Internet is the domain of spoofs and deliberately misleading material as well as containing honest mistakes. Refer to more than one source and carry out a little judicious crosschecking before taking material gleaned from the Internet as completely dependable. Of course, errors can also occur in printed sources but they are less common because printed works go through an editing and proofreading process designed to pick these up before printing.

You can generally tell from the end of the address of a website exactly what kind of organization it belongs to. Here are a few of the more common suffixes:

.ac.uk	UK academic institution
.com	commercial enterprise
.co.uk	UK commercial enterprise
.edu	US educational institution
.gov	US government institution
.net	major service provider
.org	non-profit organization

Particularly if you are not a 'web wizard', the following tips should help you quickly retrieve the information you are after:

- Speed up the process by restricting your search to the UK only. (This is usually an option offered in search engines.) If you don't find what you want, you can always search again, specifying all of the web.

- Speed up your research by restricting it, if appropriate, to a single language.
- If you are unsuccessful with one search engine, try a different one. Some search more web pages than others or work with a different database.
- If one keyword does not yield the results you want, try to think of a different keyword to use that is still related to the same subject.
- If you have a lot of searching to do, you need to be patient. Some sites can take a long time to download. Don't throw your monitor through the window: your PC is doing its best!
- The amount of time that it takes to access a website can be affected by the number of people using the Internet at any one time. If you find things are very slow and it takes an annoyingly long time to move from one site to another, you might be better to try again at a different time, when the system may be less busy. It is a good idea to avoid periods of peak use in the USA, where most Internet users live. Mornings are a good time for UK users, since this is when most of the USA will be asleep.
- Add especially useful sites to your 'Favourites' or 'bookmark' them so that you can easily and quickly return to them.
- Print out or save to disk any web pages that you are really interested in.

Your research will only be of value to you if you can actually use it when the point comes to begin writing your report. It is vital, therefore, to make a record of the things that you find out. You don't need to write out everything in full; often, you might find that you can summarize fairly lengthy passages of information using only a few well-chosen words that will trigger your memory when you read over them.

However, you do need to record enough detail to allow you to go back and check things later if necessary. Keep a list of your sources of information. It is best to make a note of titles, authors, publishers and publication dates so that you can display the information in your report if necessary (either in footnotes or in the form of a bibliography).

Some tips for successful research

- Try to make a decision early on about the type of information you are looking for, how detailed it needs to be and how much of it you need.
- Do not try to read every word of every book or article on the topic. Look at the contents page at the front of a book and the index at the back to get a quick idea of what information the book contains and whether or not it will actually be of any use to you.
- Make a decision at an early stage about the usefulness of a book or article. If it seems promising, use an appropriate reading technique to extract the relevant information. (See below for suggested reading techniques.)
- When you look something up, make written notes of facts and figures rather than trusting your memory.
- If you come across a quotation that you think you may want to cite in your report, copy it down word for word, along with its precise location, to save you having to look it up again.
- Take photocopies of articles or pages in books that you think will be useful, rather than reading them all the way through. You can read them more carefully later.
- If the book or article you are reading belongs to you or you are using photocopies or printouts from websites, you may find it easier to make notes or underlinings on the page, and use highlighter pens to mark particularly important passages. Don't do this with sources that you have only borrowed!
- In case you want to revise or check anything later, it is useful to make a note of the chapter and the section number and page number each time you copy or summarize something. If

the pages are large or the text is very dense, you might also make a note of the line number. All of this might sound time-consuming, but you will find that it pays off when you actually start writing.

Reading techniques

Most skilled readers use a variety of different techniques to extract information from books, articles and other sources. The particular technique that they use may depend on the nature of the text that they are reading and on what sort of information they are currently looking for.

The technique may even change as they progress from one part of a text to the next: they may read slowly passages that are obviously important, but rush through passages that do not appear to contain information that is relevant to their needs.

There are three ways of reading that may be appropriate when you are doing research for your report:

- skimming
- scanning
- submarine reading

Skimming

When you **skim** or **skim-read**, as the term might suggest, you are skimming over the surface of the text and reading it at speed. For example, if you flick through a newspaper or magazine or glance at a television guide, you are usually skim-reading, quickly 'getting the gist' rather than taking in every detail. It is surprising how efficient a way this can be of picking out items that are of interest while screening out all of the material that isn't.

This is an extremely useful way of gathering information, especially in our contemporary culture, where we are surrounded by sources of printed material and do not need to (or simply have enough time to) read everything closely. As you skim through a text, you can make notes of any passages that you identify as possibly requiring a more thorough examination.

Scanning

Another way of reading text rapidly is to **scan** the pages. In this case, however, you are looking for specific information, rather than trying to form an overall impression of the contents. You scan when you are looking up someone's phone number, trying to find a word in a dictionary, using the index of a book to find out about a particular subject or looking at the television listings to see when your favourite programme is on.

Perhaps you will form a better idea of the difference between skimming and scanning if you think about two possible approaches to looking at the contents page of a book or someone else's report. If you want to get a quick impression of what is there, you would rapidly skim through the contents page; if you are looking to see if a specific item is included, you would scan the page.

Submarine reading

Submarine reading is so called because this is what you do when you become completely immersed in a text. You read through it carefully, and might do a number of other things while taking in the subject matter, including analysing what is being said, comparing it with other things you have read, agreeing or disagreeing with it, rereading parts you do not understand and noting missing or incorrect information.

This kind of reading demands full concentration. You might read in this way when checking a contract, consulting an instruction manual or reading an article about a subject that you find particularly interesting.

Submarine reading is effective, but also time-consuming. A worthwhile approach combining elements of different methods is to skim through a text to identify important passages, and then adopt the 'submarine' technique for these selected passages.

Gathering all the information

Anyone doing research can tell you that a common pitfall is to become distracted by interesting but irrelevant information. You must be disciplined and keep your attention fixed on what is applicable to your subject. Don't go off on any wild goose chases.

Equally important is to have a sense of when to stop: no matter how long or detailed your report is intended to be, there will come a point when you risk having too much material to reasonably deal with. By the time you come to selecting information you will probably find that much of it is mere duplication. Keep your notes, photocopies and references in one file where you can find everything easily and keep track of how material is building up. This also applies if you are working solely on computer: create a folder for your project and store all the relevant files in that rather than have bits and pieces in different places all over your hard drive.

Using the information

Selecting information

When you feel that you have exhausted the topic in terms of research, it is time to review what you have gathered and select the material that you will actually use. This is a good point at which to remind yourself of the precise subject: keep the title of your report in the forefront of your mind.

Look at each item of information and ask yourself if it is directly relevant; discard anything that is not. Pieces of information may have caught your eye simply because they contained one or more 'trigger words' relating to your subject, but on closer examination they may turn out to be peripheral or contribute nothing of real value. Omit anything that you can identify as falling into this category. Also get rid of anything that duplicates information that you realize you already have in another form.

By the time you reach the stage of reviewing your material, you may already be forming a rough idea of the conclusions that your report will eventually reach. However, guard against the temptation to quietly drop any information that tends not to conform with these conclusions. No matter how polished and persuasive it is, your report will be worthless if it is not inclusive and impartial. The people for whom it is meant do not want to be presented with biased or incomplete information but a balanced and honest assessment in which the conclusions reached are backed up by convincing evidence.

If you are using material from a published source, you must be aware of copyright. What this means, essentially, is that an author's writings and other published works are protected by law from being reproduced without prior permission during the lifetime of the copyright holder and for the next seventy years after his or her death. Do not take the risk of prosecution: be sure to obtain written permission to reproduce copyright material before you do so, and acknowledge this permission in your final report. There may be a fee for the use of copyright material, but quite often you will find that the copyright holder will be content with a simple acknowledgement of the source.

Organizing information

Once you have narrowed the information down to what is strictly relevant, try to pick out different topics or logical lines of argument and begin to roughly divide the material according to these. This can be done in a few easy stages:

- Write down all of the arguments or points that you have assembled. You don't need to go into great detail; at this stage all you need is a brief note of each point.
- Try to collect these arguments into groups under a series of general headings.
- Now try to fit the general headings together into the most logical order. If there are arguments for and against something, group all of the arguments for it together, then do the same with all of the arguments against it. Do not allow yourself to bounce back and forth between these two groups.
- Make sure that the order you have come up with fulfils your original goals. If you can now identify any obvious gaps in the order, you may need to go back and do more research so that you can fill these in.

It is a good idea to start with a simple outline and only then move on to something more complex, fleshing out the bones only once you have built the skeleton. Don't be afraid to cross things out, put others in or move things around as you develop your plan: this is what this stage of the report writing process is all about.

As a brief example, let's return to the idea of a survey of computer printers. You will easily see that several different factors will be directly comparable, such as price, number of pages printed per minute, what range of paper sizes can be used, whether or not colours are available, how often ink cartridges have to be replaced, and so on. You can use these to form the first basic framework on which to give structure to the findings of your research. It may help you to note these down in a list:

- price
- pages per minute
- paper sizes
- colour/black only
- ink cartridge consumption

Once you have decided what the key ideas or points are, assess their relative importance and decide on the order in which you want to deal with them. There may be several different ways of arranging your material; at this point it doesn't really matter which one you choose to begin with. What is important is that your plan covers all of the material that you have so painstakingly assembled and whittled down, and that it provides a clear framework for what you have to say. Let's take as an example a report on the difference between public and private funding. Your preliminary rough plan may look something like the following:

Introduction: difference between public and private funding

1. Theoretical advantages of
   a) public funding
   b) private funding
2. Public funding
   a) Case studies: Paris, Marseille, Barcelona, Hamburg
   b) Do case studies bear out the theory?
3. Private funding
   a) Case studies: Berlin, Lyon, Madrid, Rome
   b) Do case studies bear out the theory?

Conclusion: summary of advantages and disadvantages of each system

---

Interpreting information

This is an area where your own subjective choices may come more into play. Depending on the nature of your report, simply looking at the evidence provided by the information you have amassed may well suggest what the conclusions will be. In other cases, the information could be open to different interpretations. You must be able to back up the interpretation you choose with convincing evidence.

To return to the earlier example we have been using of evaluating printers, let's say that one of the models examined seems to jam more often than others. This might indicate that it is an unreliable machine in comparison to similar models. On the other hand, it could mean that it is not being used properly: perhaps users are trying to economize by feeding it with low-quality paper. Look at the evidence carefully and evaluate it until you feel you can decide on the interpretation that convinces you.

USING THE INFORMATION

You then have to convince the readers of your report. Set out each possible interpretation of your information and say what you think about them. Balance one against another to show how you have reached your interpretation.

Running problems

During the monitoring period, Printer B was found to jam three times, while Printers A and C each jammed only once. This has obvious implications in terms of cost, time and dependability.

Printer B, however, is a relatively expensive machine intended to give a high-quality finish. It was found that jamming did not occur when a higher grade of paper was used. This argues in favour of Printer B being the best choice for prestige printing tasks.

If you follow the processes described above for each area of the information you have gathered, this will help you with the next important part of writing your report: setting out its structure.

Having established a basic plan, you may wish to expand this into a more detailed plan (see Part Two, 'Structuring Your Report'), or you may wish to move on immediately to your first draft of the report. Traditionally, at this early stage writers would use pen and paper to create a plan, adding notes and crossing things out as they went. However, word processing programs now make it easy to put down a mass of ideas and then reorder them by dragging blocks of text around your PC screen to build up a structure. Whichever method you are using, don't be afraid to change your mind: it is better to make alterations to your plan at this stage rather than later, when things are more fixed and that much harder to change and a complete restructuring might have to be carried out.

Part Two

Structuring
your Report

The basic structure

There is a typical structure that most formal reports follow (and we will look at this in detail below) but this may not be relevant for your particular needs, especially if your report is going to be on the brief side. Whatever structure you choose for your report, it may help to keep the following ideas in mind:

- Let the structure you choose be dictated by what it is you have to say and by the effect that you want to create.
- Keep the structure simple and transparent so that your readers will know what is going on and be able to follow your train of thought all the way through.
- If you are tempted to digress from the structure you have chosen, this is probably a sign that the structure isn't right and you may have to look at it again. However, once you are convinced that your structure is appropriate, stick to it throughout the writing.
- The structure should be able to accommodate all of the necessary information.
- If a piece of information does not fit into your chosen structure, this is probably because it isn't really necessary to include it. Use notes or appendices to incorporate information that your readers may find interesting but which is not essential to the thread of the argument.

While not every report needs to have an identical format, formal reports tend to follow the same basic structure. If your organization has its own 'house style' this will obviously take precedence, but you will probably find that it is unlikely to differ wildly from the structure outlined as follows:

THE BASIC STRUCTURE

- title page
- contents
- summary
- glossary
- terms of reference
- procedure
- findings
- conclusions
- recommendations
- appendices
- bibliography

The parts of a report

Title page

The title page should clearly set out the following:

- the subject of the report
- the author's (or authors') name, plus contact details
- the date of its completion.

A good title is the first and most obvious way to engage the reader's attention. Try to be concise, while still covering all the essential facts; a wordy or complex title will look to your reader like too much hard work before they even begin to read the report!

It may be that you have been assigned a specific title to use and therefore have no choice in the matter (say, *Choosing the Right Printer*), but even if this is the case you can make it more interesting by incorporating a more eye-catching, 'snappier' phrase, for example *Facts on the Page: Choosing the right printer*. However, keep in mind the level of formality required; keep it relevant and avoid being flippant.

> URBAN FOXES: Are they on the increase?
> A report by J. Renard, Chief Environmental Officer, Rowley District Council
> Rowley, September 2005

Contents

A contents page is essentially a list of all the headings and sub-headings contained in the report, ideally directing the reader to a specific page in each case. This is most important in longer pieces of work, as some readers will not necessarily want to read the whole document from cover to cover but will be keen to go immediately to those sections that particularly interest them.

Make sure that each item listed on your contents page is clearly and simply expressed. The whole point of this page is to act as a kind of signpost to what your report contains, and it should be immediately obvious to the reader where to look.

For the same reason, the order in which the contents are shown must be logical, so that readers will be guided smoothly through the list without having to go back or skip forward to find a topic that they would reasonably expect to follow on from the one before. If you have planned the structure of your report logically, this shouldn't be a problem.

Summary

Particularly in longer reports, it is always a good idea to preface the full text with a summary of its main findings. In many cases, a bit like the blurb on the cover of a book, it will help people make up their minds as to whether or not they will want to read the report itself. Obviously, while the summary should precede the main text, it will in fact be the last part to be completed. Sometimes the direction of a piece of writing changes as it is being written, and it is only when it is finished that you will be able to have the necessary overview of the whole report.

A good summary will be concise (a lengthy one largely defeats the purpose) but will include everything that is important, and set it out as clearly as possible. It could be argued that writing such a summary is a skill in itself; you may be able to write a perfectly acceptable report, but struggle to reduce your work to a summarized form. Try to adopt an objective approach to your writing, and look at it as another reader might see it. It might help you to think along these lines:

- Ask yourself what the most important points raised in the report are: what things do you regard as essential for a reader to know at the end of it?
- Make these into a brief list, expressing each as concisely as you can.
- Are there obvious links between them, with one clearly leading on to another?
- Try to construct a few grammatical sentences that will contain all of this information.
- Read over what you have written and get rid of anything that is long-winded, repetitive or otherwise inessential, making sure the text still flows naturally.

Here is an example of a summary:

Summary

This report was commissioned by the Gotham Academy of Art to investigate the responses of students to different teaching environments and the effectiveness of these environments. It was conducted over one full session in Autumn 2006, with a class of 24 students representing the sample studied. Its main findings are:

- · 90% of the students sampled enjoy formal lectures and feel they are useful learning environments
- · 60% of students think that smaller tutorial groups are useful learning environments
- · 50% of students consider field trips to be worthwhile
- · 30% of students consider individual study to be valuable

The report concludes that these results largely demonstrate that the current mix of teaching environments is the right one, while making a recommendation that field trips are looked at with a view to making them more relevant to students' needs.

In some cases, especially when the report is exceptionally long and detailed, a specific kind of summary may be required, known as an executive summary or abstract. The difference between this and an ordinary summary is that it is long enough to stand as a document in its own right, ranging from one or two to as many as a dozen pages but never more than around a tenth of the full document. It is essentially intended for the use of those who are too busy to devote the time to reading the document in full but who still may have to take decisions based on its main findings.

Glossary

You might find that in your report you have to make use of words, phrases or abbreviations that are very specialized or highly technical. It may be that those who are going to read your work will already be familiar with these kinds of reference, if, on the other hand, you believe that the report will be seen by non-specialists or people from outside its particular field, then it is essential to include a **glossary**. The word comes from a Latin term meaning 'to explain'. A glossary is simply an alphabetical list of specialized terms that you have used in the text followed by brief definitions: a sort of mini-dictionary.

Try to explain your terms clearly and concisely and, as far as possible, in simple everyday language. Don't fall into the trap of using one specialist term to define another: you will leave the reader none the wiser. A common error among amateur glossary writers is to mix up the different parts of speech. Don't define a verb as if it is a noun, or vice versa.

   ✗ ***brainstorming***   *to have an intensive group discussion to generate new ideas*

✔ **brainstorming** *an intensive group discussion intended to generate new ideas*

✘ **downsize** *reducing the size of a workforce*

✔ **downsize** *to reduce the size of a workforce*

If you are unsure about the different parts of speech, refer to the relevant section on pages 69–77. Meanwhile, here are a few more examples of brief and clear glossary entries:

bullet point	*one of several important pieces of information in a list, each introduced by a large black dot*
cartridge	*the container for ink in a printer*
FIFO	*acronym for: first in, first out*
reprographics	*the reproduction of graphic or typeset material*
toner	*powdered pigment used in a photocopier*
USP	*abbreviation for: unique selling point*

A good tip is to compile your glossary as you are writing. This means that you will be defining the terms while they are fresh in your mind. It also avoids the chore of having to search the whole report at the end; apart from anything else, you might miss some. When you have completed your report you can go back to your glossary and make any necessary refinements.

Terms of reference

This section should briefly state:

- the subject of the report
- the scope (and limitations) of the report
- why the report was written
- who asked for the report
- who was responsible for writing the report
- when the report was completed

While the subject of the report should be simple enough to state, it may be less easy to define its scope. However, if you bear in mind the most important items that are covered, and make clear what is NOT included, it should be straightforward enough to set this out. The 'why', 'who' and 'when' should also pose no difficulties. Below is an example of typical terms of reference.

> *This report was commissioned by Bigsplash Publicity to compare and contrast the effectiveness of Internet pop-up advertising and the traditional mailshot, with a view to identifying the optimum method for use in publicizing a new line of health drink to be launched in 2007. It was compiled by J. Watson and F. Donnelly and its findings were presented in March 2006.*

Procedure

The purpose of this section is to make clear what methods were used in gathering the information on which the report's findings are based. The important thing here is to show that the methods used are reliable and likely to yield dependable and accurate information. It will be obvious to the experienced eye whether or not this is the case. A report's conclusions may turn out to be what those who asked for it want to hear, but if the findings have not been arrived at by reliable and objective methods, they will know that the conclusions are essentially worthless.

It is also useful to the reader to know how long the author spent on compiling the information. Readers will want to be assured that the author has not taken a superficial or hurried approach but has taken time to gather and sift all possible evidence. Don't take the risk of giving your readers the impression that you have jumped to conclusions!

Many methods of gathering information have already been discussed under 'Research' on pages 22–31, but it is useful to list the most common here:

- meetings and visits
- interviews
- published reference sources
- personal observation
- questionnaires and surveys
- scientific measurement

Not all of the above will be relevant in every case, but some of them are bound to have been used in even the most brief reports.

> *This report is based on the following sources of information:*
> - *interviews with a sample of members of the public, both Internet users and non-Internet users*
> - *questionnaires issued to sample group, both by mail and on line*
> - *guidelines issued by the Advertising Standards Authority*

Findings

This, of course, is the real 'meat' of any report and it is bound to be the longest and most detailed part of it. It is vital that all of the relevant information is presented here. This information must be clearly set out, using headings, subheadings, distinct paragraphs, and so on. It must also be logically argued, from preliminary findings to sensible deductions, all backed up by reliable evidence and explanatory examples. There must be no bias shown here by the writer of the report but rather an even-handed analysis of the facts that have been ascertained.

It is a good idea to lay out the findings in a formal pattern, both for the writer's sake, by helping to organize the material, and for the reader's ease of reference, making it very clear what is being discussed. To take an example, let's assume our report is entitled 'School trips: are they worthwhile?'

---

1   A look at costings
1.1 Breakdown of costs per student for sample Primary schools
1.2 Breakdown of costs per student for sample Secondary schools
1.3 Costs for Primary parents
1.4 Costs for Secondary parents
2   What do head teachers have to say?
2.1 Survey of a cross-section of Primary head teachers
2.2 Survey of a cross-section of Secondary head teachers
3   What do teachers accompanying trips have to say?
3.1 Interviews with sample of Primary teachers
3.2 Interviews with sample of Secondary teachers
4   What do students have to say?
4.1 Interviews with Primary school students
4.2 Interviews with Secondary school students
5   What do parents have to say?
5.1 Results of questionnaires distributed among parents of Primary students

---

5.2 Results of questionnaires distributed among parents of Secondary students

6 A look at Health and Safety implications

6.1 Identifying minimum teacher/pupil ratio

6.2 Study of regulations, guidelines and procedures

The system of numbering shown above is not the only possible method, but it is certainly common and widely recognized. We could just as easily have used letters as labels for the main divisions, with roman numerals for the subdivisions:

A. A look at costings

A (i) Breakdown of costs per student for sample Primary schools

A (ii) Breakdown of costs per student for sample Secondary schools

A (iii) Costs for Primary parents

A (iv) Costs for Secondary parents

B What do head teachers have to say?

We might also have used a different combination of numbers and letters, as in:

I. A look at costings

I (a) Breakdown of costs per student for sample Primary schools

I (b) Breakdown of costs per student for sample Secondary schools

I (c) Costs for Primary parents

I (d) Costs for Secondary parents

II. What do head teachers have to say?

As long as the material is set out clearly it doesn't really matter which system of labelling is used. The important thing is that the reader can easily see the relationships between the different elements of the findings and how one part of the material follows on from another. Try not to break the findings down into too many subdivisions (such as 2.2 (a) (i), for example). Confronted with this kind of over-the-top labelling, a reader might grow irritated by constantly having to refer back to the main division, or may be completely put off by the prospect of navigating through such dense flagging! If you are tempted along this path, stop and look again at your material. Ask yourself if the distinctions you are keen to make are really that marked, or if it is the case that only someone as close to the material as you are can see their validity. Try using a simple paragraph break or new line to indicate a slight change of emphasis; this is often enough. It is better to maintain a smooth rhythm of prose, moving smoothly from one item to the next, rather than present a jerky, bitty piece of work.

You may well find that you feel the need to expand on some particularly important point, or offer the reader more in the way of explanation of some of your findings: how do you do this without interrupting the main thrust of the argument too much? The best method is to use a system of notes.

... examined by the Hirst Committee[2] of 2005 ...

2. Chaired by Hazel Hirst, Managing Director of Hirst and Gautier PLC, this committee surveyed a range of methodologies currently in use in the private sector in various areas of England and Wales. See bibliography under 'Hirst Report'.

These notes can be footnotes, which are placed at the bottom of the page where they occur, usually in a smaller size of type, or endnotes, which are gathered in one place, at the end of the text. There are no hard and fast rules as to which system to use. However, if you have only a scattering of notes, it is more convenient for a reader to find them on the relevant page. On the other hand, if you find you can't avoid having several notes on each page, it is probably tidier to gather them together at the end rather than having text pages of wildly varying length with masses of small print at the bottom. It is important that your notes should be identified in a logical and obvious sequence:

> 1, 2, 3, …
> 1a, 1b, 2, 3a, 3b, 3c, 4 …
> (i), (ii), (iii), …
> (a), (b), (c), …

You don't have to use numbers to flag up your notes, of course. Especially if you have only a few notes, you can use symbols, such as asterisks and daggers, singly or in multiples:

> *
> **
> §
> †
> ‡

A similar approach should be taken to illustrations such as diagrams or charts. If there are not too many of these it is perfectly acceptable to include them among the findings. Make sure that they are clearly numbered or labelled in sequence as they occur, and check that they are directly referred to in the text, rather than leaving them to appear seemingly at random.

> *Diagram 1: Comparison of ink cartridge replacement requirements of three leading printers.*

Diagram 2: Average temperature for the month of July in Leeds, 1955–2005.

Table A: European Parliament political affiliations as at 1 August 2006.

Table B: Temperature conversion scale, Fahrenheit to Celsius.

However, too many illustrations will tend to break up the text to a point where you risk distracting the reader from the main thrust of your argument. In this case it is better to gather all of your diagrams, tables and charts at the end of the report under the 'Appendices' section and simply refer the reader there from the relevant point in the main text.

Conclusions

If there is one section of a report that is more important than its 'Findings', it is the conclusions. To put it simply, this is what the report was commissioned for, the whole point of the exercise of researching and writing it. It is vital, therefore, that the conclusions are presented as clearly and straightforwardly as possible. It must be obvious to the readers what the report has come up with, otherwise your time (and theirs) has been wasted.

It is really about reminding the reader of the facts that have already been looked at, but drawing all the strands of the argument together, emphasizing what you consider to be the most important discoveries. This is your chance to demonstrate that you have not simply plucked some idea out of the air because it appealed to you, but can show logically how what you have found leads you to your conclusions.

This is not the place to introduce any new material or evidence that you have not already discussed. The reader will certainly not expect this to happen and it is bound to lead to confusion if it does. If you find, by the time you are setting out your conclusions, that you suddenly feel there is more to say, don't say it here but go back to the 'Findings' section and deal with it there.

Don't forget that many busy people will not be prepared to devote much time to reading a whole report but will simply head straight for the conclusions to try to find out exactly what they want to know. There is no point in resenting the fact that they're blithely skimming over your hard work and missing the chance of revelling in your peerless prose! Just make sure that you are giving them an accurate and concise summation of your fuller discussion, without unnecessary repetition or long-windedness.

While clarity is all-important, the style you use is largely up to you. You may want to sum up the matter in a few discursive sentences:

On the whole, most head teachers in both Primary and Secondary schools in the sample examined are very much in favour of school trips. They emphasize that there must be an educational purpose to such trips but tend to recognize the importance of extramural experience that may not normally be available to students.

Similarly, most teachers feel that such trips are valuable and are happy to devote their time to running them. Parents, too, are mostly in favour, and feel that their financial contribution is money well spent.

Students, both at Primary and Secondary levels, focus less on possible learning outcomes and tend to be more interested in having an enjoyable time in the company of their peers, but most of those who have been on a school trip react positively and would be happy to repeat the experience.

Teachers have been made aware of all Health and Safety implications and a significant number hold First Aid qualifications. A pool of parents has offered its services to ensure that the adult/pupil ratio does not go below 1:5.

On the other hand, you may want to use a more formal and statistical approach:

---

1. Among Primary head teachers surveyed, 95% were in favour of school trips; among Secondary heads the figure was slightly less, at 89%.

2. 99% of Primary teachers sampled were in favour, with 78% of Secondary teachers in agreement.

3. 100% of Primary school students interviewed were happy with school trips; the figure drops to 89% among Secondary students.

4. Of the questionnaires returned by involved parents, 93% of those with Primary-age children showed approval of school trips; the figure was 91% among parents of Secondary students.

5. 41% of Secondary teaching staff holds a First Aid qualification, while the percentage among Primary school teachers was 57%.

Now, you may well think that since you have reached the 'Conclusions' you must have concluded. Not so; there are still important areas to be covered before you can consider your report to be finished.

Recommendations

This section is where the report writer must decide whether or not specific actions are to be recommended. It may be that this is not part of the original brief and that those who commissioned the report do not want such suggestions but prefer to decide for themselves. Some types of report (for example, technical reports, progress reports, minutes, etc) will not require any kind of recommendation to be made. However, in many cases recommendations will be expected.

While this represents the point at which the writer comes closest to expressing personal opinions, nothing should be recommended that is not demonstrably suggested by the report's conclusions. Make it clear how the findings of the report logically lead you to your recommendations. Again, it is a mistake to try to introduce new material at this point. If recommending actions leads you into areas you have not already covered, go back and deal with them in the body of the text, so that they do not strike the reader as an unwarranted new development.

> The following courses of action are recommended:
> 1. The new invoicing procedure should be rolled out companywide as soon as possible.
>
> 2. Brief training seminars in implementing the new procedure should be held for account managers.
>
> 3. All major customers should be alerted to the possibility of slight delays in invoice payment until the new system is bedded in.
>
> 4. A follow-up review of how the new procedure is working out should be conducted after six months.

Don't worry if you feel that no actions can be usefully recommended. It is perfectly possible that the findings of your report lead to the conclusion that the status quo is just fine. If that is the case, say so frankly (as long as you can back this up).

Appendices

This section is where you gather together all of the illustrative or supporting material that is too long, too detailed, too technical or too digressive to appear in the main body of the report. This can include tables, diagrams, graphs, charts, maps, drawings, photographs, or lengthy extracts from other publications.

If you have a lot of material to include in this section you should make it easier on the reader by dividing different types of material into separate appendices, keeping all diagrams together, for example, or all documents. Each appendix should be clearly labelled in sequence.

Appendix 1
Appendix 2

Appendix (a)
Appendix (b)

and so on.

You should let the reader know about the existence of this material by flagging up references to it in the appropriate places in the main text:

The figures for the southern region (Table 5, Appendix A) show that promotional events can have a significant effect on sales.

A recent French survey (See Appendix C) has shown that public tastes have diversified even further than these results would suggest.

In this way, the reader is given the opportunity to look more closely at your sources and the evidence you are drawing conclusions from. But if they are happy to take this information at face value they need not digress from the main text of the report.

If you have used endnotes, then this section is the place to include them. Set them out in the order they appear in the text (which should be apparent if you have numbered or labelled them in a clear sequence). For example:

Notes

1. *Of 250 questionnaires issued, 234 were returned.*

2. *The time period was October 2005 to January 2006.*

3. *See Table A in Appendix (i).*

Bibliography or references

Use this section to list all of the sources of information that you have used. Don't mention any that you looked at but drew nothing from: you might think this will impress others with the breadth of your research, but there is always the chance that your report will be read by those who can tell that this is only padding.

For a relatively short or less formal report it should be enough to list your sources alphabetically. However, if several different types of source have been used (such as questionnaires, surveys and personal interviews), it makes sense to split them into separate groupings for the reader's convenience.

For a longer, formal report it is better to follow a structured style of listing sources. If there is no house style to be applied, the most widely adopted method is that known as the Harvard System or the author–date system. Under this system, sources are listed in alphabetical order of the author's surname, and there is a set style for each element of the reference:

- the author's surname, followed by forename(s) or initials
- the year of publication
- the title (if the source is a book, its title should appear in italics or with an underline; if the source is an article, give its

title (again in italics or underlined), followed by the title (in roman type) of the periodical or book in which it was published)

- the number of the edition of the book, if applicable
- the name of the publisher, along with the place where the publisher is based

For example:

Singh, V., 2002, *The Key to Statistics*, 2nd edition, Mansell Press, Oxford.
Spaulding, Captain G., *African Exploration in the early 20th century*, Geography Today 147, pp. 15-27.

With the increasing use of the Internet, it may well be that some of your sources will not be printed publications but websites. To avoid confusion, keep these in a separate section, headed, for example, Internet or Web resources. Alphabetical order may be difficult to apply, but you will not go far wrong if you simply list these in the order in which they appear in the report, along with the date when you accessed them.

http://www.statsworld.com/singh/key.html accessed 27/10/06
http://www.geogday.com/147/africa/spaulding.html accessed 7/11/06

Now that we have looked at each of the various elements of a report in some detail, it would probably help to draw all of the strands together if we can see an example of everything in its place in a complete report. Obviously, there is not enough space here to include a lengthy piece of writing; instead, what follows is an example of a fairly brief formal report. As you will see, not all of the report sections discussed above are relevant (such as summary or bibliography) and are therefore not included.

To: Pamela Pacitti, Managing Director
From: Jack McRae, Training Manager
Date: 18 November 2006
Subject: Provision of in-house training courses

1. Introduction
The purpose of this report is to examine the feasibility of holding all future training courses in house. External training providers were consulted, estimates of training costs were sought and received, and comparative costs were examined. Questionnaires were completed by 80 employees from four different departments, and 10 of the respondents were subsequently interviewed by members of the training department.

2. Advantages
2.1 Following consultation with four of the company's regularly used external training providers, it was calculated that in-house training would bring about a reduction in the present cost of 26% in the first year (see Appendix A).

2.2 It was felt by 65% of the staff that training courses could be better designed to suit the specific needs of the organization, and therefore bring immediate benefit to the company as a whole.

2.3 45% of those who responded to the questionnaires felt that they were more likely to participate in training courses if they were held on site.

3. Disadvantages

3.1 Some respondents, particularly in the sales department, expressed their concern that valuable business contacts arising from participation in external training courses would be lost if all training was to be held in house.

3.2 Some training needs are very specific, and may be required by only a relatively small number of members of staff. It was felt that these needs could not always be met by in-house training courses, as the necessary expertise could not always be brought in from outside the organization.

3.3 Participation in external training courses is seen by 30% of respondents as a perk of the job, and it was felt that the important motivational element of this would inevitably be diminished if all training were to be provided in house.

4. Conclusions

As a result of the analysis of the advantages and disadvantages of providing all training in house, the following conclusions may be drawn:

· Considerable savings will be made in the immediate future if in-house training courses are introduced.
· The staff response is favourable overall, particularly at the higher levels of management, although in some departments the absence of external training courses is seen to be a real disadvantage, because of the loss of potential business contacts.
· While many employees feel that introducing in-house training would be a positive move and would probably lead to increased participa tion, 30% regarded it as a loss of a perk.

5. Recommendations

In view of the above conclusions, my recommendations would be:

· In-house training courses should be introduced where a significant number of participants will be required to attend.
· In cases where there are fewer than five participants, external training courses should continue to be an option.
· Members of staff should be consulted regularly as to their level of satisfaction with in-house training courses. Their feedback should be taken into account, especially regarding motivational factors, and addressed.

Part Three

Good Report Writing

Getting started: drafting Getting started: drafting
Getting started: drafting
Getting started: drafting

Getting started: drafting

In Part Two we looked at the structure common to most types of report. With this structure in mind, or at least your own rough version of it, you are probably ready to start writing. Unless you are so confident in your own abilities that you can accelerate from zero to finished report in one go (in which case, you probably don't need this book!), this is the point at which you will produce your first draft.

It is a good idea to get through this stage as quickly as possible, so make a start without assuming that the first thing you write will necessarily still be there in your final report. The important thing is to get started. It is far easier to make changes once you have something to work with, rather than wasting time staring anxiously at a blank sheet of paper or an empty screen and wondering what to do and how to get it right first time.

Once you make a start on writing, you should find that the preparation and planning work that you have already done begins to pay off and the writing begins to flow more easily. Keep in mind the following points as you write:

• Follow the plan that you have drawn up according to the guidance given in Part One. It would be a shame to waste all the work that you put into producing it, and the plan will help you to marshal your ideas.

• Move forward steadily from paragraph to paragraph, giving each point as much attention as it merits. If one paragraph turns out to be especially short, check whether the point that you are making in it is actually worth making on its own, or whether it could be incorporated in another paragraph or even deleted altogether. On the other hand, if a paragraph turns out to be especially long, you might want to split it up. Ask yourself if the point being made in it is actually important enough to merit being covered in more than one paragraph.

- Don't assume that you have to complete each paragraph perfectly before moving on. If you get stuck at any point, go on to the next paragraph and come back to the problematic one later. You will then be able to look at it with fresher eyes and perhaps spot what needs to be changed. If this doesn't help, and you are really stuck, delete the offending paragraph and start it again.

- It is likely that new ideas, connections and insights will occur to you as you write. If new ideas do present themselves, don't be afraid to 'go with the flow' and change what you are doing to take account of them, provided that they can be smoothly accommodated within your plan.

- Try to complete the discussion of a point in one place rather than leaving it and coming back to it later. Otherwise, you could risk presenting a 'bitty' argument or letting the reader lose the drift. You might even forget to come back to it yourself! If you have no alternative but to leave a point and return to it later, be sure to let your readers know exactly where the discussion will be completed, as in: *We will return to the question of fish stocks when we come to discuss the environmental factors.* Once you have completed your report you can go back and insert the relevant section number to which it refers, eg *See section 3.6.*

- Try to deal proportionately with the various different points and arguments. Don't spend a long period of time handling one single point and then skirt around other points that are equally, if not more, important.

- Think about the people who are going to be reading your report and try to do what you can to make life easy for them. If people are going to look at your report to retrieve information, think about making it easy to scan by using headings, lists and tables. If people are going to read it as a continuous piece, try to make sure that it is divided up into manageable paragraphs and that there is a coherent and logical structure.

- If you make a statement or express an opinion, remember to always back this up with evidence in the form of facts and figures or quotations. However, be careful to use facts and figures selectively and appropriately. There is no point in overwhelming your readers with them.

For many people, being asked to write a report may represent being faced with the first serious piece of writing that they have had to contemplate since leaving full-time education. This can be a daunting prospect. Writing essays is one thing; writing a piece that is important to your professional life is entirely another. After all, the people who read your report are putting not only your own competence and reputation under scrutiny but perhaps also those of the company and organization that you represent.

Obviously, you will want to make a good impression, and while you may have complete mastery over the subject matter, have all the relevant facts and figures at your fingertips, and know exactly what you want to say, it may be that your writing skills will let you down when the time comes to put everything down on paper. Perhaps it doesn't seem very important to you, but you will find that many people who will be looking at what you have written will be put off by sloppy grammar, poor or inconsistent spelling, or a dense and confusing layout of text. This can be enough for them to refuse to take your work seriously or even reject it altogether as not being worth the waste of the valuable time necessary to get through it. Wouldn't it be a shame if an important message was lost because the medium wasn't up to scratch?

This book is about report writing, and that will be the focus throughout. However, in this section we are going to look at what constitutes good writing in general, how to achieve this, and how this applies to the writing of reports. You may think that you don't need this; if you don't, that's all well and good. Nevertheless, most of us could do with a refresher course in writing from time to time.

We are going to look at the nuts and bolts of writing good English, or, if you like, take the machine apart and see what makes it tick before putting it back together so that it runs better than ever! Let's begin with grammar.

Grammar

Some people shy away from the very thought of grammar, writing it off as that boring stuff that they used to try to teach you at school but which now (thankfully) you don't have to think about any more. This may be true in many contexts, but not when you have a report to write.

What grammar does is give language a structure and this is essential to getting the meaning across. It is important to know the rules of grammar and to follow them. Imagine trying to play a game of football if there were no hard and fast rules and every participant played in whatever way they thought fit. The result would, of course, be chaos, leaving no clear picture of what is going on. This applies to writing good English too: if we all know and follow the same set of rules we will all be able to write in a way that makes sense to others and equally be able to read and understand what others write.

Even if you have planned and drafted your report by hand, you will almost certainly be using a computer to produce the final version. You can let a word-processing program (such as Microsoft Word) check your grammar for you as you write. If you choose this option a green wavy line will appear under grammatical constructions that the program considers questionable. Be careful, however; this kind of grammar check (and the same applies to automatic spellchecking) is not infallible. The best method is to use these checks to suggest possible errors, which you can then check using your own knowledge of grammar and make corrections if you wish. In any case you should still read the final version carefully to check for grammatical errors. If you are at all unconfident about your command of grammar, the following section will guide you through the fundamental points.

It is vital in any sort of writing to write in proper sentences. Do you know what constitutes a sentence?

Sentences

A sentence is the expression of a particular thought. For that reason, it should be self-contained and able to stand on its own. In precise terms, a sentence should begin with a capital letter, contain a **verb**, and end with a **full stop**. (See the sections on 'Parts of speech' on pages 69–77 and 'Punctuation' on pages 78–90.) Look at this example.

> *The meeting was attended by a representative from each department.*

This is a simple sentence which conforms to the rules. There are more complex sentences, however.

> *The meeting was called to consider three matters: finance, materials and schedule.*

As you can see, this sentence has two distinct parts. While the first part could stand on its own and make sense, the second could not. As it lacks a verb, it is not a sentence but a *phrase*. It is easy enough to construct a sentence if you follow the rules. The next step is to put a number of sentences together to form a paragraph.

Paragraphs

A paragraph is a subdivision of a longer piece of writing. The main reason for dividing something into paragraphs is to make it easier to read. Long stretches of unbroken type will tend to put off even the most determined reader, and can lead to what should be separate points being lost or confused. A paragraph is a useful pause for a reader, and equally useful for a writer, but don't be tempted to throw paragraph breaks in at random, just to break up the look of the page. An experienced reader will expect the paragraph divisions to mark a transition from one point to another and will be confused if this is not the case.

How do you know when to start a new paragraph? It should be clear to you when you are moving, however slightly, from one idea or aspect to another. This is the time to end one paragraph and begin another. Don't let your paragraphs grow too long; equally, don't have so many that your text begins to look like a collection of unconnected thoughts. A new paragraph is usually signalled by beginning on a new line, sometimes with the left edge of the line indented, sometimes without this but with a blank line in between (as in this book).

Parts of speech

Words are the components from which a clear and understandable sentence is built up, and it is important to be able to distinguish one type of word from another, or, in other words, the different parts of speech. Here is a list of the most common parts of speech used in English:

- noun
- verb
- adjective
- adverb
- pronoun

- preposition
- conjunction

Noun

A noun is a word that gives the name of something, whether it is an object (such as a book or a brick), a living creature (such as a woman or a beetle), or a concept (such as trust or terror). There are different varieties of nouns, each performing different functions, but for the purposes of report writing we will consider just the following two. A proper noun is the name of a particular person or thing, and will always begin with a capital letter: *Elizabeth*, *Poland*, *Christmas*, *Springsteen*, *Edinburgh*, *Mars*, *Swahili*, *Nissan*. A common noun is the name of a type of thing rather than any individual, and does not begin with a capital letter: *girl*, *country*, *festival*, *musician*, *city*, *planet*, *language*, *car*.

Verb

A verb is a word that signifies an action, experience, occurrence or state.

action	*eat*, *sing*, *run*, *die*, *type*, *stumble*
experience	*feel*, *hate*, *suffer*, *understand*, *mature*, *become*
occurrence	*snow*, *explode*, *dawn*, *flower*, *darken*, *crumble*
state	*be*, *live*, *remain*, *continue*, *evaporate*, *melt*

Like nouns, verbs can take different forms. The form of a verb changes according to person, number and tense. There are three persons in verbs: the first person (*I*), the second person (*you*) and the third person (*he*, *she* or *it*). Let's look at the verb *camp*. The first person form of this verb is *I camp*; the second person form is *you camp*; the third person form is *she camps*. This is straightforward enough, but it is further complicated when the number of people comes into account. *I camp* is the first person singular; the first person plural form is *we camp*. In this case, the second person plural form is the same as the singular: *you camp*. The third person plural, however, is *they camp*.

Now we add the concept of tense to the equation. The tense of a verb tells you at what time the action takes place. Something happening in the present tense is happening now: *we are camping*. Something that has already happened requires the past tense: *we camped*. The future tense expresses something that has not happened yet: *we will camp*.

We have used the verb *camp* as an example because it is what is called a regular verb; that is, its various forms follow simple set patterns. Some verbs, though, are irregular and do not follow predictable rules. For example, the past tense of *eat* is *ate*; the past tense of *be* is *was*; and the past tense of *shine* is *shone*. These irregular verbs are one of the things that makes English fairly difficult for foreign-language speakers to learn. As they follow no rules they just have to be learned.

Verbs can be even more complex than we have seen above, but, as many will no doubt be happy to learn, the more subtle variations belong to a more in-depth study than is needed here.

Adjective

An adjective is a word that describes another word. It tells you something about the other word, such as its quality, class or colour. Colour is easy enough (*the red shoes*; *a blue sky*; *green leaves*). By class, what is meant here is a category or type, which can be what something is made of (*a tin cup*; *leather sandals*;

ceramic tiles), its shape (*a square box*; *round glasses*; *curved arms*), or nationality (*French bread*; *Italian shoes*; *American aircraft*). Quality is concerned with the particular nature of something (*a short journey*; *sad stories*; *the old lady*).

Some adjectives can take different forms, especially when they are used in comparing things. These forms are called comparative and superlative:

ADJECTIVE	COMPARATIVE	SUPERLATIVE
small	*smaller*	*smallest*
ugly	*uglier*	*ugliest*

Some forms cannot be made by simply adding *-er* or *-est*:

ADJECTIVE	COMPARATIVE	SUPERLATIVE
wonderful	*more wonderful*	*most wonderful*
ridiculous	*more ridiculous*	*most ridiculous*

There is a great deal more to be said on adjectives, but as long as you have a clear grasp of the basic information above, they should not give you many problems when you are writing your report.

Adverb

The easiest way to remember what an adverb is for is to think that it *adds* to a *verb*; that is, it tells you something more about the verb it is connected with:

	VERB	ADVERB
The boy	**walked**	**quickly**
The sun	**shone**	**brightly**
She	**sang**	**well**
Everyone	**laughed**	**heartily**

Things that an adverb can tell you about an action include *when* it was/is being done (*We arrived yesterday*), *how* (*It rained heavily*), *how much* (*She misses him terribly*), *where* (*I ran home*), and *how long* (*The lecturer paused briefly*).

As you can see, most adverbs end in *-ly* but not all do. Also, don't assume that a word that ends in *-ly* must be an adverb; words like *homely*, *surly*, *lively* and *costly* are actually adjectives. Like adjectives, adverbs can have comparative and superlative forms:

> *I'll be back soon.*
>
> *You'll be back sooner if you hurry.*
>
> *Whoever's back soonest can put the heating on.*

However, some forms cannot be made by simply adding *-er* or *-est*:

> *Did we play well?*
>
> *Yes, but they played better.*
>
> *We'll see who plays best in the final.*

Again like adjectives, many adverbs (especially those ending in *-ly*) form comparatives and superlatives by adding *more* or *most*:

I can't see clearly.

Can you see more clearly with glasses?

I can see most clearly in bright sunlight.

Try to spend your time usefully.

Your day off would be spent more usefully in tidying up than going to the pub.

The people who are the least bored are those who spend their time most usefully.

Pronoun

Essentially, a pronoun is a word that is used to take the place of a noun. Why should one word have to take the place of another? For one thing, it saves the trouble of tediously repeating something:

I met Nina and asked her if she wanted to come to the party.

This is obviously better than:

I met Nina and asked Nina if Nina wanted to come to the party.

Imagine having to repeat all those 'Ninas' over and over again!

The noun that a pronoun stands for can also be plural:

I met Nina and her sister and asked them if they wanted to come to the party.

A pronoun can also take the place of a much longer phrase:

> When I met Nina she was wearing a lovely new black leather jacket with silver buttons, and I asked her where she bought it.

There are various types of pronoun and you will find a detailed breakdown of them in any good grammar book.

Preposition

A preposition is a word that is used to join phrases and add some information about them. The following examples show prepositions in use and how different ones convey different information:

> We live in Newcastle.
>
> We live at the bottom of the street.
>
> We live near the river.
>
> We live down the street from you.
>
> We live on next to nothing.
>
> We live under the flyover.
>
> We live next to your cousins.
>
> We live above a shop.
>
> We live over there.
>
> We live between the Singhs and the Russells.

There is an old rule of grammar that forbids ending a sentence with a preposition, as in: I've got quite enough to put up with or How much is it going for? However, while some purists insist that a preposition must always come before the word or phrase it is connected with, in practice sticking obsessively to this rule will make what you are trying to say sound over-formal or even silly, as in *I've got quite enough with which to put up* or *For how much is it going?* As with many points of language, common sense will often tell you where to draw the line.

Conjunction

A conjunction is a word used to join two statements or phrases, making a longer sentence rather than having a shorter, more disjointed effect. The most common simple conjunctions are *and* (which signifies that something is being added), *but* (which introduces a contradiction or reservation of some kind), and *or* (which suggests a choice or alternative):

> *egg* and *chips*
>
> *He was very conceited* and *would never listen to criticism.*

> *harsh* but *fair*
>
> *It was a tiring day* but *a very satisfying one.*

> *tea* or *coffee*
>
> *You can fly there* or *go by train.*

A slightly different form of conjunction is used to add a piece of information relating to an existing statement, but which is unable to function as a sentence in its own right (a subordinate clause). These include *if, unless, although, because, since, until*.

> *It'll be a grand day out* if *the rain stays off.*
>
> *It looks like we've failed,* unless *anyone has a bright idea.*
>
> *The project turned out to be a great success* although *it didn't seem so at the time.*

There is no point in going now, because *it'll be done before we get there.*

This has been a fairly quick look at the basic points of grammar. There are lots of grammar rules, not all of which are directly relevant to the practice of report writing. The most important ones are those that help you to write clearly, and these will stand you in good stead no matter the field of writing. The subject has other, often more complicated, aspects but for the purposes of this book the above should be enough to deal with most problems or confusion.

Punctuation

When we speak we tend to pause in certain places, sometimes to give special emphasis to certain words or phrases, sometimes to separate different units of information and sometimes to show that we are moving from one idea to another. Other factors such as facial expressions, tone of voice and even hand gestures also come into play as devices that we can call on to help communicate our meaning. In print, however, none of these things are applicable and they have to be replaced by the conventions of punctuation.

Perhaps you don't think punctuation is all that important, and that people who make a fuss about it are just being nit-picking. Have a look at this example:

> *me and my pals hate that sort of music it is rubbish everybody knows that were daft about franz ferdinand what more can I say*

What is wrong with the words above? Apart from anything else, we can't clearly understand what is meant because of the lack of punctuation. Let's try a few different approaches:

> *... ... ... It is rubbish. Everybody knows that we're daft. About Franz Ferdinand, what more can I say?*

> *... ... ... That sort of music – it is rubbish everybody knows. That were daft about Franz. Ferdinand, what more can I say?*

> *Me and my pals hate that sort. Of music, it is 'Rubbish everybody!'*

This is going a bit far, of course, but the point needs to be made that proper punctuation is essential to getting your meaning across. In this section, we're going to take a look at the different punctuation marks and how to use them to the best effect. The main punctuation marks are:

- full stop
- question mark
- exclamation mark
- comma
- colon
- semicolon
- dash
- brackets
- quotation marks
- apostrophe

Full stop

The full stop (or period, as it is also known, especially in the USA) is a simple dot, used to mark the end of a sentence.

> *The sun has gone down. Now the creatures of the night begin to stir.*
>
> *In the morning we had a presentation by the head of Human Resources. After that we had tea and coffee.*

Note that the next letter after a full stop must be a capital.

Question mark

The question mark is self-explanatory: it signals the asking of a question.

> *How are you?*
>
> *When is the next train?*
>
> *Could I have another cup, please?*
>
> *Who cares?*
>
> *What's the difference between a buffalo and a bison?*

Note that a question mark indicates the end of a sentence, just like a full stop, and should be followed by a capital letter. Be sure that what you are writing is indeed a question. Look at this example:

> *I wonder what the time is?*

Do you see anything wrong here? Many people assume that a sentence beginning with I wonder must be a question and accordingly end it with a question mark. In fact, the sentence is not a question but a simple statement of what you are wondering:

> *I wonder what the time is. Excuse me, do you have the time?*

Exclamation mark

An exclamation mark is used to end a sentence in a dramatic way, to show that what has been said is out of the ordinary in some way, such as being important, surprising or comical.

I love you!

Don't forget to save your work before you log out!

This new product is turning out to be a disaster!

Don't fall into the trap of using too many exclamation marks, as this will weaken their effect. You don't want your report to look like a comic book; neither do you want to come across as overly excitable. The fact is that in formal report writing there are likely to be relatively few genuine cases where an exclamation mark is appropriate. Remember that, like a full stop or question mark, you will have to follow an exclamation mark with a capital letter.

Comma

The comma is a highly useful and versatile piece of punctuation. It marks a place where there is a pause, or separation between things, that is not as firm or absolute as a full stop.

Looking back on it, it was a useful exercise after all.

The report concluded, among other things, that until we were in full possession of the facts it would be too risky to commit ourselves to any single product, no matter how attractive, economical or readily available it might be.

It can be used between items in lists:

A4 paper, manila envelopes, compliments slips and other stationery or between adjectives:

> *a long, slow, fascinating journey*

It can separate parts of a sentence, marking off material that could be omitted and still leave a sensible statement:

> *Her findings were surprising, if not totally unexpected, and we had to adjust our plans accordingly.*

> *The department took delivery of new PCs, the first for two years, just before Easter.*

> *I can e-mail the details later or, if you prefer, put them in the post.*

If you use commas as a kind of parenthesis, they must go in pairs; don't forget the second one.

Colon

A colon is used to separate one piece of text from another, not as finally as a full stop, but more as an introductory pause leading to a separate but connected statement.

> *The answer was obvious: diversify or go out of business.*
> *What are you trying to say: that there is no hope?*

or to introduce a list of things

> *Choose one of the following options: bold, italic, roman.*

Different parts of a title can also be separated by a colon.

> *Last-Chance Saloon: the decline of the traditional pub.*

Semicolon

You might find it helps to think of the semicolon as 'half a colon'. It indicates a separation or pause, not as marked as that of a colon or a full stop, but stronger than that of a comma. It can separate two parts of a statement, where this is required, but without divorcing them entirely:

> *Many candidates sit this exam; most of them fail.*
>
> *Discipline had grown slack; consequently, absenteeism was rife.*

It also comes in handy for separating elements in a list that is too complex for commas to do the job:

> *We are going to be looking at the following categories: domestic sales and marketing; overseas sales and marketing; product launch budgets; and returns policy.*

Dash

The dash can be a useful means of breaking up text. It can be used, like commas, as a means of parenthesis:

> *You will find a list of sources consulted – including websites – on page 127.*

But again, like commas, don't forget the second, closing one. A dash, like a colon, can also introduce a list or anything that follows on from what has already been said:

> *We need to look at three main areas of transport – air, sea and rail.*

> *The report was rather controversial – but the truth often is.*

Some people feel that using dashes instead of commas or colons is inelegant. This is not necessarily true, but they should not replace them completely, and they should not be overused to the point where they are practically the only punctuation visible.

Brackets

While commas and dashes can be used for parenthesis, the best and clearest way of marking off text within a sentence is to use brackets:

> *We will deal with this (and any other competent business) at a later stage.*

> *Several people have contributed (see a list of names below) and their efforts are much appreciated.*

> *Now is the time to finish any project(s) you are currently working on.*

> *The idea of the 'global village' was developed by Marshall McLuhan (1911–1980).*

By using brackets you are essentially signalling to the reader that what they contain is not essential and that your main point could stand without it; nevertheless, you are reminding them that this information exists and may be useful to them. Don't forget the closing bracket.

Quotation marks

Quotation marks (often shortened to quotes) are also known as inverted commas. Their primary function is to show that what they enclose represents words that have been spoken:

> *When we asked if he was prepared to take part in our survey, 'No way,' was all he said.*
>
> *"The half-year results are most encouraging," announced the CEO.*

As you can see, quotation marks can be double or single. If there is no house style for you to follow, the choice of form is up to you. In general terms, single quotation marks are used most in British English, while in American English double quotation marks tend to be the norm. Be sure, however, to be consistent whatever option you choose.

Another slightly different use is to indicate something that is slightly different from its surrounding text. This may be because you are referring to a word or phrase that is well-known and perhaps not completely formal:

> *Is this the end of 'Dress-down Fridays'?*
>
> *I'm calling just to 'touch base' with you.*

or intended to be humorous or not to be taken literally:

> *Another pessimistic forecast from 'Happy Larry' in Budgeting.*
>
> *We went for 'a quick drink' after work.*

or you want to indicate that you are doubtful about the truth of the statement in question:

> *Gerry came out with yet another of his 'hilarious'
> stories.*
>
> *If you sign up for a year you get a 'free' gift.*

It used to be common to use quotation marks to indicate the *title*
of a play, film, painting or other piece of work:

> *We went to see 'West Side Story' at the Lyceum last
> night.*
>
> *He resurrected his career by appearing in 'I'm a
> Celebrity, Get Me out of Here'.*

However, this use of quotation marks has largely been replaced
in typed documents by the use of italics or underlined type.

Are you ever irritated by people who pepper their speech with
'quote, unquote' or make those wiggly signs in the air with their
forefingers? You might say they're doing something useful ... by
reminding you to close your quotation marks!

Apostrophe

You have to be careful with apostrophes. A lot of people misuse
them, and a lot of people get quite worked up about that.
Apostrophes are primarily used to show possession of something:

> *Asha's car*
>
> *the government's majority*
>
> *Is that Dave's sister?*
>
> *women's issues*

Note that if a word ends in *s* and you want to make a possessive form of it, you simply add the apostrophe on its own:

> *girls' coats*
>
> *our friends' houses*
>
> *lovers' meetings*

Now, here are some examples of wrong formation of the possessive:

✗ *your's* (should be *yours*)

✗ *her's* (should be *hers*)

✗ *their's* (should be *theirs*)

✗ *it's* (should be *its*; see below for proper use of *it's*)

Another use of apostrophes is to show that something has been missed for the sake of abbreviation:

SHORT FORM	FULL FORM
I'm	*I am*
I'd	*I would* or *I had*
I'll	*I will*
it's	*it is* or *it has*
wouldn't	*would not*
(s)he's	*(s)he is* or *(s)he has*
should've	*should have*
fish'n'chips	*fish and chips*
three o'clock	*three of the clock*
'70s	*1970s*
ma'am	*madam*
who's	*who is* (don't confuse this with *whose*)

If you have a problem deciding whether to use *its* or *it's*, it might help if you try to remember that you should only use an apostrophe if, in your sentence, you can substitute *it is* or *it has*.

We've all seen the handwritten signs in grocers' windows or on chalked pub menus where 's has been used to make a plural form:

   ✗ *tomatoe's*

   ✗ *mussel's in white wine sauce*

A shop sign that proudly announces itself as *LET'S GALORE* may think it is telling the world that it has plenty of properties available for letting, but what it is actually doing is suggesting we should all 'galore' together (whatever that may be). Try to remember that, as a rule, you should *never* pluralize words in this way. There are exceptions, such as *mind your p's and q's*, but these are few and it is better to err on the safe side.

Hyphens

Finally, a brief word about hyphens. These should be used sparingly; their main purpose is to avoid ambiguity:

   There were forty-odd people there.

rather than

   There were forty odd people there.

But do take care when you are positioning them. There is a world of difference between

✗ *Her dress had three quarter-length sleeves.*

and

✔ *Her dress had three-quarter length sleeves.*

If you are uncertain whether to hyphenate certain compound words, such as *lifejacket* or *website*, then a good dictionary will advise you.

Using capital letters

There are certain occasions when capital letters should always be used. These include:

- at the beginnings of sentences:

    This is the dawn of a new age.

    She started her new job yesterday.

    What is the delivery date?

- at the beginnings of proper names:

    His name is George Jones.

    Manchester is his home town.

    She speaks fluent Italian.

- at the beginnings of titles:

    Among the guests were Lord and Lady Dempster.

    Her ambition is to become Prime Minister.

    You should bring this to the attention of the Chief Executive Officer.

This dress belonged to the late Princess Grace of Monaco.

World War II.

- in certain abbreviations:

  He became Governor-General of the BBC.

  Several MPs voted against the bill.

  HIV positive

  The TUC annual conference

- the first person pronoun:

  I can't make it this evening.

  You and I were made for each other.

- the deity:

  I hope to God it isn't true.

  Thank God.

Spelling

Some people insist that correct spelling isn't important, and that it is rather pedantic to get too hung up on it; it is the meaning that matters, after all. While this may be all very well in the world of personal correspondence, whether by e-mail or text messaging, in report writing or any other form of business writing spelling *does* matter. If you want what you have written to be taken seriously by those it is aimed at, your report should be presented in as polished a way as possible.

For many people, bad or inconsistent spelling indicates sloppiness at best; at worst, lack of intelligence. If your writing shows that you can't be bothered to check or correct your spelling, perhaps you also couldn't be bothered to check your facts. If you want readers to do you the courtesy of actually reading the fruits of your hard work, you might at least do them the courtesy of making it as easy as possible for them to read. If they have to puzzle over words whose meaning is unclear they are quickly going to lose patience. Don't give a busy person the excuse to throw your work aside simply because it is too much trouble for them to read it.

Think of it in these terms: how much faith would you put in a statistical document that had obvious arithmetical errors in it? Why, then, expect others to put credence in a report that isn't correctly spelled? To resurrect an old cliché, if a job's worth doing, it is worth doing properly. That applies as much to spelling as to anything else.

SPELLING

You might ask, what about computer spellchecks: don't they make all of this unnecessary? The straight answer is: not really. A spellchecking program is only as good as the source it is derived from; you might find yours is based on an American dictionary, and there are plenty of differences between US and English spelling (see pages 96–98). A spellcheck will pick up words that are entirely wrongly spelled, but it will accept a wrong spelling if that happens to match a word in its dictionary. For example, if you meant to type *meter* (as in *electricity meter*) but accidentally key *metre* (ie the measurement) no spellcheck will point out the mistake. Apart from that, if you happen to write something that is really nonsense (and we all have our 'off' days!), such as *sodium waterfall above the blue nylon trousers*, your spellcheck will find nothing to flag up.

Some spellchecks even have the facility called predictive spelling. What this means is that if you type only the first letters of a word, the remainder of the word will automatically be filled in for you. Be very wary of this: some highly ludicrous constructions can end up in your writing if you blithely let this happen without checking the results carefully. Use a spellcheck if you must, but with caution, and don't blindly accept its every suggestion.

A good dictionary is the best guide to spelling, and it will show you how to form plurals and different verbal parts. You might wonder how you can look up a word that you don't know how to spell. The only answer is to keep looking until you find what you want. If particular words give you trouble, note down their correct spelling and make sure you familiarize yourself with them.

Some people seem to be naturally good spellers; others definitely need a little help. There is not enough space here to go into all of the complexities of English spelling, and there are plenty of books available that will do that for you if you really need it; what is offered here is intended as a balanced survey of the general rules. It may not be enough to let you go on and win a spelling bee, but it should help you to steer clear of basic errors.

Forming plurals

Most plurals are formed simply by adding an *s* to the end of the basic word:

toy becomes *toys*
book becomes *books*
girl becomes *girls*

but words that end in *s* or an 's-like' sound take *-es*:

fuss becomes *fusses*
rush becomes *rushes*
fax becomes *faxes*
touch becomes *touches*

Some words ending in *f* or *fe* change their endings to *-ves* in the plural:

hoof becomes *hooves*
life becomes *lives*

but not all:

chief becomes *chiefs*
roof becomes *roofs*

Words ending with a consonant followed by *y* change to *-ies* in the plural:

baby becomes *babies*
cry becomes *cries*
curry becomes *curries*
city becomes *cities*

Be careful with words ending in *o*. Some of their plurals simply add an *s,* but others take the form *-oes*. Often, it is just a matter of getting to know and remember which does what; check a dictionary if in doubt.

studio becomes *studios*
stereo becomes *stereos*
video becomes *videos*

but

potato becomes *potatoes*
tomato becomes *tomatoes*
hero becomes *heroes*

Some plurals are completely irregular, but the most common examples of this are learned early and not usually forgotten:

foot becomes *feet*
woman becomes *women*
child becomes *children*

Some reflect the fact that they have been borrowed from a language other than English and still obey the rules of their original language:

criterion becomes *criteria*
phenomenon becomes *phenomena*
crisis becomes *crises*

analysis becomes *analyses*
cactus becomes *cacti*

Again, if in doubt consult your dictionary.

Forms of verbs

The most straightforward verbs are those with an infinitive (the base form of a verb, from which other forms are made) to which -*s*, -*ing* and -*ed* are added to create the verb forms:

> *fear*
> *fears*
> *fearing*
> *feared*

> *I work*
> *She works*
> *We are working*
> *They worked*

For many verbs, however, it is not that simple. For example, verbs whose infinitive ends in a consonant need to have that consonant doubled when -*ing* or -*ed* is added:

travel	*drop*	*refer*
travels	*drops*	*refers*
travelling	*dropping*	*referring*
travelled	*dropped*	*referred*

Infinitives that end with a silent *e* drop it when -*ing* or -*ed* is added:

95

smile	bore	use
smiles	bores	uses
smiling	boring	using
smiled	bored	used

Infinitives that end in -y are more complicated. The final y changes to i except for the form ending in -ing:

apply	deny	copy
applies	denies	copies
applying	denying	copying
applied	denied	copied

You should remember that these rules are for general guidance and such is the nature of the English language that there are always exceptions to them. When in doubt, consult a dictionary, and try to commit exceptions to memory when you come across them.

Differences between British and American spelling

It may be that the research for your report will lead you to publications or websites that are American in origin. You should bear in mind that there are a few basic differences between US and UK spelling and avoid using the former in a British English context. This may not seem very important to you, especially as you often find American spellings gaining acceptance in Britain, but many people value British traditional spelling and will be put off or distracted from what you want to say if your report is peppered with too many Americanisms. If you are relying on a computer spellcheck, make sure it is set for English (United

Kingdom), not English (United States). These are the basic rules governing the different spellings:

- words ending in *-our* in UK English will end in *-or* in US English
- words ending in *-re* in UK English will end in *-er* in US English
- words that can end in *-ise* or *-ize* in UK English will always end in *-ize* in US English

UK SPELLING	US SPELLING
armour	*armor*
candour	*candor*
favour	*favor*
honour	*honor*
labour	*labor*
centre	*center*
fibre	*fiber*
litre	*liter*
theatre	*theater*
apologise or *-ize*	*apologize*
emphasise or *-ize*	*emphasize*
realise or *-ize*	*realize*

Apart from these rules, there are various other differences. A few of the more common variations are listed below.

UK SPELLING	US SPELLING
anaemia	anemia
anaesthetic	anesthetic
axe	ax
cancelled	canceled
catalogue	catalog
cheque	check
dialogue	dialog
doughnut	donut
jewellery	jewelry
plough	plow
programme	program
sceptic	skeptic
sulphur	sulfur
traveller	traveler
tyre	tire

Commonly misspelled words

We all have our weaknesses in spelling, particular 'blind spots' that we can't avoid making mistakes with. It is as if we have committed the wrong spelling to memory and can't replace it even though we know it is wrong! All you can do is try to remember your own recurrent misspellings and look out for them.

However, there exists in English a body of words that are spelled wrongly more often than any others. The table below lists a number of these in alphabetical order (correctly spelled!) for you to check against. You might find it helpful to go through the list and pick out any that you find particularly troublesome and try to memorize them.

abbreviation
abscess
absence
accelerator
accessible
accidentally
accommodation
achieve
acquiesce
address
advertisement
aerial
aeroplane
aghast
almond
annihilate
argument
asphyxiate
assassinate
asthma
athlete
autumn
bachelor
beautiful
believe
berserk
biscuit
blancmange
broccoli
business
calendar
catarrh
ceiling

cemetery
changeable
chaos
character
committee
competition
connoisseur
conscientious
consensus
correspondence
courteous
definitely
deliberate
description
desperate
diarrhoea
dilemma
diphtheria
disappear
disappoint
doubt
draughty
ecstasy
eczema
embarrass
embodiment
encyclopedia
environment
exaggerate
exceed
excellent
excerpt
exercise

exhaust
exhilarating
experience
fascinate
fluorescent
foreign
friend
fulfil
gauge
genuine
ghastly
ghost
glamorous
gorgeous
gorilla
government
grammar
guarantee
guard
guilty
gymkhana
haemorrhage
handkerchief
harass
height
honorary
humorous
hygiene
hypocrisy
idiosyncrasy
illiterate
immediately
independent

SPELLING

indispensable
innocuous
inoculate
instalment
interrogate
irrelevant
irresistible
jealous
jeopardy
jewellery
jodhpurs
khaki
knowledgeable
laughter
leisure
leopard
liaise
lieutenant
liquefy
liquorice
maintenance
manageable
manoeuvre
marriage
martyr
mayonnaise
medicine
millennium
miniature
minuscule
miscellaneous
mischievous
misspell

mortgage
moustache
naïve
necessary
neighbour
niece
noticeable
nuisance
obscene
occasion
occurrence
opportunity
parallel
parliament
peripheral
permanent
perseverance
pharaoh
phenomenon
phlegm
physics
playwright
pneumonia
precede
prejudice
privilege
proceed
professor
pronunciation
psychiatry
psychology
publicly
pyjamas

questionnaire
queue
rarefied
receipt
receive
recommend
reconnaissance
refrigerator
remember
reminiscence
repetition
reservoir
restaurant
rhinoceros
rhyme
rhythm
righteous
sacrilegious
satellite
sausage
scissors
secretary
seize
separate
sergeant
sheikh
sheriff
shriek
siege
sieve
silhouette
sincerely
skilful

solemn	susceptible	verruca
soliloquy	technique	villain
sovereign	temperature	weight
spaghetti	tomorrow	weird
sphinx	tranquillity	wholly
squabble	truly	woollen
suave	turquoise	wrath
subterranean	twelfth	yacht
subtle	unfortunately	yield
succeed	unwieldy	yoghurt
success	vacuum	zealous
succinct	valuable	zoological
supersede	vegetable	
surprise	vehicle	

A large number of proper nouns and names are also continually misspelled. Here is a list of some of those that are frequently the cause of mistakes. As with the list of commonly misspelled words, try to memorize those that you tend to have difficulty with.

Abu Dhabi	Cincinnati	Guinness
Achilles	Connecticut	Gurkha
Aer Lingus	Curaçao	Hawaii
Afghanistan	Dáil Eireann	Hogmanay
Alzheimer's	Daiquiri	Inuit
Azerbaijan	Dobermann	Jekyll
Baghdad	Don Quixote	Kalashnikov
Bahrain	Edinburgh	Kazakhstan
Beaujolais	Eisteddfod	Liebfraumilch
Beijing	February	Llandudno
Buddha	Filipino	Llanelli
Burkina Faso	Gandhi	Machiavellian
Caribbean	Gomorrah	Marylebone

SPELLING

Massachusetts
Michelangelo
Mississippi
Montessori
Morocco
Odyssey
Oedipus
Pavarotti
Pepys
Philippines
Pinocchio
Plaid Cymru
Pompeii

Portuguese
Pythagoras
Qantas
Renaissance
Rhesus
Riyadh
Rothschild
Schwarzenegger
Shi'ite
Sikh
Sinn Fein
Taoiseach
Thessaloniki

Trossachs
Tutankhamen
Ulysses
Versailles
Wedgwood
Wednesday
Weimaraner
Widnes
Wodehouse
Yom Kippur
Zimbabwe

Dealing with special information

The standard rules of grammar, punctuation and spelling will stand you in good stead for writing your report. There are, however, some things that you might want to include that are not easily dealt with under these rules and will require special attention. We're going to look at how to deal with:

- speech
- quotations
- proper names
- abbreviations and acronyms
- numbers
- dates
- lists
- foreign words and phrases
- words used in an unusual sense

Sometimes there are precise conventions governing the presentation of these things. However, sometimes the way that such information is presented might depend on your own choice, or on the preferred style of the particular organization for which you are creating your report.

If you are not following a house style, it is always worthwhile to keep a record of the decisions you make about these types of material in particular situations. This will help you to achieve consistency and make sure that the same style is used throughout your report.

Speech

If the speech is only reported, and the actual words are not given, then quotation marks are not used:

> *She said there must be a marked improvement in performance the following year.*
>
> *He asked what was wrong with this year's figures.*

Although this is generally the style adopted in reports, on occasion you might want to show the actual words spoken by someone. If you are doing this, place the words inside quotation marks:

> *'There must be a marked improvement in performance next year,' she said.*
>
> *'What's wrong with this year's figures?' he asked.*

Any punctuation marks that belong to the quotation should be included within the quotation marks:

> *'I am hurt,' said Jim, 'and I need help.'*

In this sentence, the comma after *hurt* is part of the speech, and so it is included within the quotation marks.

Punctuation that applies to the surrounding sentence stands outside the quotation marks:

> *'I think', said Jim, 'you should go and fetch help.'*

In this sentence, the speaker would have made no pause between *think* and *you*. Therefore, the comma after *think* is not part of the speech and so is not included within the quotation marks.

When a speech finishes before the end of the sentence, do not use a full stop at the end of the speech, but use a comma instead:

> *'That is a beautiful car,' said Hugh.*

When the end of the speech is also the end of the sentence, there is no need to put a full stop after the closing quotation marks:

> *Hugh said, 'That is a beautiful car.'*

Quotations

Quotations can be useful in a report. For example, you might think it is more vivid and authentic to quote the actual words used by someone in one of the interviews that you conducted as part of your research process. Also, it can save time and space to give quotations from books or articles rather than paraphrasing what they say. Always be sure to identify any quotation properly as such and attribute it accurately to its source.

Here are some tips on how to deal with quotations.

Short quotations can be incorporated directly into the surrounding sentence, within quotation marks:

> *Shakespeare said that 'all the world's a stage'.*

Unlike in speech, the final full stop is placed outside the quotation marks.

DEALING WITH SPECIAL INFORMATION

If you use quotations that run to several sentences or several lines of text, these should begin on a new line and be slightly indented. Long quotations should be preceded by a colon, but there is no need to use quotation marks:

> *This point is clearly made by Daniel, who asserts that: Grammarians do not impose rules on a language; they merely collect from the language rules already in existence, and set them forth in an orderly way.*

Italics may be used to highlight particular words or phrases within a quotation. If you do this, you must tell the reader that this is not in the original text by adding '(my italics)' at the end of the quotation:

> The report said that their activities 'extended beyond what was acceptable and *could pose a threat to national security*' (my italics).

Proper names

It is always worth the effort to try to get the presentation of proper names right. Particularly with people's names, think of it as a form of courtesy to them. It can cause needless offence if you get proper names wrong, and why risk alienating readers when a little care is all it takes?

Capital letters are used at the beginning of a proper noun such as the name of a person or place:

> *This is my friend Mark Keiran. He lives in Milton Keynes.*
> *We've had this e-mail from Ashoq in Aberystwyth.*

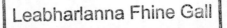
Leabharlanna Fhine Gall

Some words can be used both as proper nouns and common nouns. These words are written with capitals when they refer to the *title* of a specific individual, event, movement or institution, but not when making more general references:

PROPER NOUN	COMMON NOUN
A statement by the Prime Minister	*when she became* prime minister
The European Parliament	*the* parliament *of Europe*
When she joined the Communist **Party**	*when she became a* communist
World War I	*those who fought in both* world wars

You will sometimes come across proper names written without capitals, for example when a company or organization wants its name to appear informal and contemporary; a name might even run words together without spaces, in the style of an e-mail address:

> *learndirect*
>
> *creativescotland*

The titles of books, periodicals, plays, films, albums, TV programmes, long poems and works of art are indicated either by italics or quotation marks.

The first word and all significant words that follow it begin with a capital letter:

The Lord of the Rings

Beneath the Planet of the Apes

The band played 'This Old Heart of Mine'.

Foreign names and places may have different forms in English and the local language. Use the English forms where these are more familiar than the local names: it will sound less affected to write *Cologne* rather than *Köln* and *The Hague* rather than *Den Haag*. However, many local versions have now become accepted as the standard English form. For example, *Mumbai* is now preferred to *Bombay* and *Beijing* is preferred to *Peking*.

Words such as *river*, *ocean*, *valley*, etc take a capital first letter when they form part of a proper name:

> *the Ohio River*
> *the Pacific Ocean*
> *the Thames Valley*

Many place names are not spelled with an apostrophe, even though you might expect there to be one:

> *St Albans*
> *Earls Court*

In other place names, however, the apostrophe is used:

> *Land's End*
> *St John's Wood*

Most place names that involve a preposition will be spelled with a hyphen:

Stoke-on-Trent

Weston-super-Mare

Because the spellings of place names often do not conform to consistent rules, you should make a point of checking the correct form of any that are unfamiliar to you before you commit them to print in your report.

Abbreviations and acronyms

Abbreviations are simply groups of letters that represent a word or group of words. They are mainly used because they are more economical of space and time than repeating the full form on each occasion that it turns up. If you use an abbreviation in your report, make sure you explain it the first time it appears.

> *You will be reporting directly to the CEO (Chief Executive Officer) in the first instance.*
>
> *What is the APR (annual percentage rate) on this loan?*

Alternatively, you could define it in your glossary.

Abbreviations can be written using lower-case letters (*asap, pm, mm, oz*), upper-case letters (*BC, EU, CNN*) or a combination of the two (*Hz, pH, BSc*). There is often a question as to whether or not to use a full stop after an abbreviation to indicate that letters have been omitted. In modern British English, full stops are generally not used in the following cases:

- after a shortened version of a word (*Dr, Mr, Prof*)
- after abbreviations of countries or organizations (*UK, EU*)
- after scientific symbols (*kg, cm*)

Full stops are optional but are becoming less common in cases such as these:

- after strings of letters representing words (*eg* or *e.g.*; *ie* or *i.e.*; *RSVP* or *R.S.V.P.*)
- after people's initials (*H.G. Wells* or *HG Wells*)

If you want to create a plural form of an abbreviation, you may be unsure about whether or not to add the letter s at the end. Different people use different approaches, but if in doubt the following general guidelines will keep you from going far wrong:

- Do not add *s* to metric units (*76cm*, *786g*, *500cc*).
- For most other units, it is normal to omit the final s, but in some cases it is perfectly acceptable to include it (*100yds*, *24hrs*).
- A few abbreviations are pluralized by doubling the abbreviation instead of adding *s* (*pp = pages*).
- It is acceptable to use an apostrophe when creating a plural of a lower-case abbreviation (*p's and q's*).
- However, do not use an apostrophe to create a plural form of an upper-case abbreviation (*MPs*, *AGMs*, *CEOs*).

An acronym is slightly different from an abbreviation. It is similar because it too is formed from initials or parts of other words, but the difference is that it is treated like a proper word and pronounced like one (*NATO*, *LAN*, *Oxfam*, *coed*). As with abbreviations, don't assume that everyone knows what a particular acronym stands for: either explain it the first time you use it or put it in your glossary.

Numbers in text

Numbers come into many reports when the writer has to deal with statistical or technical material. Try to bear in mind that not all of your readers may be 'mathematically minded' or particularly keen to plough through great swathes of statistics. You may want to confine your statistics and tables to appendices, while summing up what they mean in verbal form within the text itself. Whatever approach you adopt, make a point of helping your readers by presenting numbers as clearly and consistently as possible.

The most commonly used way of writing numbers in text is to show the numbers between one and twelve in words, but to use figures from 13 onwards. The preceding sentence is an example in itself, but here are two more:

> *She has three children.*
>
> *a journey of 35 miles*

The exception to this rule is that it is always better to spell out a number in words if it comes at the beginning of a sentence:

> *There were 16 of us on that course.*

but

> *Sixteen of us attended that course.*

Always use figures when numbers are part of measurements (*16cm*, *77°C*), including percentages (*57%*) and times of day (*7.45pm*), as well as when expressing a person's age (*He will be 75 on Saturday.*).

Use words for birthdays and anniversaries:

his eighteenth birthday

their fortieth wedding anniversary

Numbers that consist of more than one word are usually written with a hyphen:

a cheque for twenty-one pounds and eighty-seven pence

She was thirty-three on her last birthday.

Where possible, fractions should always be expressed as a single symbol (¾, 4½) rather than as a keyed sequence of characters (*3/4, 4 1/2*). When they are written out in full, fractions should be hyphenated:

two-thirds

five and three-quarters

If you need to include very large numbers in your report, use commas to make them easier to read. To decide where to place the commas, count from the right and place a comma after every three figures:

a crowd of 23,678

a population of 167,983

2,569,746 square kilometres

The exception to this is that in science books or articles the preference is for four-figure numbers to be closed up:

9000

and for numbers above four figures to have a thin space instead of a comma:

> *10 000*

You may well have to include **dates** in your report. Here are some guidelines to follow.

When writing dates out in full, show them without commas and without a suffix after the number of the day:

> *13 November 2007*

If you want to use dates in a shortened form, the British style is to use the order day/month/year:

> *My date of birth is 13/11/64.*
> *The conference runs from 26/5/06 to 5/7/06.*

Be aware that the American style is different, using the order month/day/year (This is why the destruction of the World Trade Center on September 11 2001 is referred to as 'nine-eleven', rather than 'eleven-nine'):

> *My date of birth is 11/13/64.*

If there is any possibility of confusion, write the month in words and the year in full:

> *My date of birth is 13 November 1964.*

When referring to historical dates, the usual style is to use small capitals when indicating whether a date is BC or AD:

AD 56

700 BC

(The letters AD strictly should always be placed in front of the number of the year, but in practice they are often placed after the number.)

If you place AD before the number of the year, this means *in the year of our Lord*, and so you do not need the word *in* to be included in the phrase:

He was born AD 56.

Some organizations, such as museums, prefer to use the abbreviation CE (meaning *Common Era* or *Christian Era*) instead of the more formal abbreviation AD (in Latin = *Anno Domini*). Check your house style if you have one.

When referring to approximate dates, use the abbreviation *c* (which is short for the Latin *circa*, meaning 'around'). Note that this is always followed by a full stop, and that it refers only to the date coming immediately after it. For example, when giving the years of someone's birth and death:

c.1604–c.1683 (this means that both dates are uncertain)
c.1604–1683 (the date of birth is uncertain, but the death date is known)
1604–c.1683 (the date of birth is known, but the death date is uncertain)

When writing the names of decades, you can use figures (*the 1990s*, *the 90s*) or words (*the nineteen-nineties*, *the nineties*) and there is no need to use apostrophes. It doesn't matter which option you choose, but try to be consistent and use the same form throughout your report.

When writing the names of centuries, it is customary to use ordinal numbers expressed as figures:

> *the 21st century*
>
> *the 2nd century* BC

If you want to use the century as an adjective, to label something as belonging to that century, a hyphen is needed:

> *19th-century architecture*
>
> *early 20th-century blues*

You can use an abbreviated form, which is created by using a lower-case *c* to mean 'century' after the number, or by using an upper-case *C* before the number:

> *C19*
>
> *18c–19c*
>
> *19c architecture*

If you are working to a house style, it will usually give guidance on the presentation of numbers; otherwise, following the rules above should satisfy most requirements.

Lists

The chances are that you will want to include a list or two in your report. When a list is used in any piece of continuous writing, you can make the structure clear by:

- using a form of introductory wording that establishes directly that a list is to follow
- using a colon immediately before the start of the list
- separating each item of the list with commas or semicolons
- presenting each item in the list in an equivalent manner

The neatest way of separating the items on a list is to use commas, provided that the commas are not already present in the text:

> *The ideal candidate should have the following qualities: exceptional creativity, a passion for promoting healthy eating, experience in working as part of a team and the ability to work under pressure.*

If the items on the list are longer or more grammatically complex, it is better to use semicolons:

> *The committee made several main recommendations: firstly, that a new post of Creative Director should be established; secondly, that the existing post of Managing Editor should be abolished; finally, that the company should seek to relocate to more suitable premises.*

For long or complex lists, rather than writing a solid paragraph it is possible to separate the items, giving each a line of its own. This will, of course, take up more space, but it has the advantage of making the list that much easier to read:

> *The successful candidate will require:*
>
> *a degree or other higher education qualification;*
>
> *the ability to speak persuasively to all levels of management;*

teamworking skills;

experience in research;

energy, enthusiasm and commitment.

With the increasing trend in modern English usage towards informality, simplicity and minimal use of punctuation, it is becoming more usual to use bullet points to indicate the items on a list and use a very open style of punctuation:

The ideal candidate should be:

- *exceptionally creative*
- *passionate about promoting healthy eating*
- *highly experienced in working as part of a team*
- *able to work under pressure*

Another style for presenting a list is to use numbers or letters instead of bullet points. This style is appropriate when the items on the list are ranked in order of importance or when numbers will be useful for referring to the items later on in the text:

Contestants will receive credit for:

(i)   technical ability

(ii)   artistic interpretation

(iii) innovation

Whichever style of list that you choose, check that the introductory wording correctly runs on to each of the listed points:

The ideal candidate should be:

✔ *exceptionally creative*

   ✔ *passionate about promoting healthy eating*

   ✘ *have experience in working as part of a team*

   ✘ *have the ability to work under pressure.*

Foreign words and phrases

If possible, you should avoid using foreign words and phrases in report writing. They tend to make your writing difficult to understand and can appear pretentious. As has been said before, anything that has an off-putting effect on the reader is best omitted.

However, if you find that there is no way round using such a word or phrase, the following can be taken as general guidelines.

The English language contains many words that have been borrowed at one time or another from other languages, including ones from Greek, Latin, French, Spanish, Italian, German and Dutch. However, most of these have become 'naturalized' and are now regarded as standard English words. It is not necessary to give any special treatment to words such as *aficionado* (which was originally Spanish), *croissant* (which was originally French), *graffiti* (which was originally Italian) or *zeitgeist* (which was originally German).

You may be able to tell when a foreign word has become naturalized; the most common signs are:

- It becomes pronounced in a more English-sounding manner.
- It becomes widely used in English sentences.
- It is listed in English dictionaries without italic letters or a label that indicates its foreign status.

If a foreign word or phrase has not been naturalized and you find that you have to use it, it should be shown in a different typeface to the surrounding text: italic when the rest of the sentence is in normal roman type, but in normal roman type when the sentence is in italic.

She had to admit the idea had a certain *je ne sais quoi* about it.

He administered the coup de grâce *to the ailing company.*

If you feel that you need to give the reader an immediate translation, this should appear in brackets and in the same typeface as the main part of the sentence:

The principle of *caveat emptor* (let the buyer beware) is enshrined in law.

We met in a kafenio *(coffee house) in Athens.*

The title of a film, piece of music or other work of art may come from another language:

She used a quotation from *Le Misanthrope* to illustrate her point.

If there is no recognized English title for the work, give any translation of the title in quotation marks:

He appeared in La Verdad Sospechosa *('The Suspicious Truth').*

If there is a recognized English equivalent, treat the title of the translation as a work in its own right, and put it in the same typeface as the foreign title:

The publication of Im Westen Nichts Neues (All Quiet on the Western Front) *caused a sensation.*

DEALING WITH SPECIAL INFORMATION

If you need to write French words, take care to show any accents correctly. French words might include grave accents (*père*), acute accents (*sauté*), circumflex accents (*bête noire*) or cedillas (*garçon*).

If you need to write German words, include any umlauts (*Führer*). German nouns always begin with a capital letter.

If you need to write Spanish words, include tildes (*mañana*) and accents showing stress (*olé*).

Foreign words that have become naturalized in English may sometimes retain an accent from their original language. This is often because the accent helps to show how the word is to be pronounced, or helps to distinguish it from a similar English word. The following are some of the most common examples you are likely to want to use:

à la	*dénouement*	*papier-mâché*
après-ski	*divorcé(e)*	*pâté*
blasé	*émigré(e)*	*piña colada*
café	*fête*	*première*
cause célèbre	*fiancé(e)*	*protégé(e)*
cliché	*frappé*	*purée*
communiqué	*matinée*	*rosé*
crèche	*mêlée*	
déjà vu	*née*	

Some naturalized French words have different masculine and feminine forms. In most cases, the feminine form is created by adding an *e* to the masculine form:

MASCULINE FORM	FEMININE FORM
blond	*blonde*
divorcé	*divorcée*
émigré	*émigrée*
fiancé	*fiancée*
protégé	*protégée*

Words used in an unusual sense

There are times when you may want to alert your readers to the fact that a word is being used in an unusual or special way. You can draw attention to the special use of a word by putting it in italics or by putting quotation marks around it.

For example, you might want to show that a word is being used in a way that is rather different from its standard meaning, such as in a technical sense rather than the everyday one:

> *Since last month we have counted over 5,000 'hits' on our web page.*

You might wish to alert your readers to the fact that a word is being referred to, not for its basic meaning but as a particular word:

> *I strongly object to the use of 'traitor' in your letter.*

You might think that the word you are using is likely to be unfamiliar to many of your readers, but no real alternative is available to you:

> *He specializes in bowling leg breaks and 'chinamen'.*

DEALING WITH SPECIAL INFORMATION

In some cases, you might want to show that you are using a word only because someone else has already used it, it is not a word that you would normally use, and that you don't fully approve of it:

> *The top came off and a kind of sticky 'goo' came out.*
>
> *No doubt the new CEO will be keen to 'downsize' the company.*

Italics are always used in preference to quotation marks when you want to give special emphasis to a word:

> The evidence only came to light *after* the trial.
>
> The letter should have been addressed to *Ms*, not *Mr* Ahmed.

Vocabulary

Your vocabulary is the range of words that you know and normally use. Each person has one, and each is different, depending on such factors as education, reading habits, profession and so on. When you consider the vocabulary available in the English language (just look at the size and contents of a good desk dictionary.) you will appreciate how much is available to you. How is this important in report writing? Two important ways are in being interesting and in being precise.

Obviously, you want those who read your report to be interested by it and willing to read it all the way to the end. One way to help achieve this is to avoid being dull, and one of the dullest features of any piece of writing is stale or repetitive language. Look at this example:

> The XRT789 is a good printer, one of the best printers in its price range. You can get it to print in black and white and colour and be sure to get good reproduction. It takes a big range of paper sizes but isn't too big to fit on the desktop. With this printer you will get nice results at a nice price.

Not exactly inspiring, is it? The information you want is all there, but it is presented in such an uninteresting way that you would be forgiven for being less than excited. Let's look at the piece again, with no changes other than in the vocabulary used.

> The XRT789 is an excellent printer, one of the most versatile printers in its price range. You can use it to print

*in black and white and colour and be sure to obtain fine
reproduction. It takes an extensive range of paper sizes
but isn't too bulky to fit on the desktop. With this printer you will achieve first-rate results at a competitive
price.*

As you can see, the second version uses exactly the same sentences and phrases, the only difference being the replacement of
vague repetitious adjectives by varied and precise ones. This is
not to say that there is no place for simple direct language or that
you must use a fancy word where an everyday familiar one will
do; far from it. But it is worth the effort to try to think about what
exactly it is you want to say and how best to express it. What is
accepted (and hardly noticed) in conversation or e-mails is not
necessarily acceptable in a formal piece of writing.

To return to the example, 'good' is a perfectly useful word, but
does it say everything? What is it about this printer that makes
it good? In this case, if it is the range of jobs that it can do then
'versatile' is not only more expressive but more precise. Similarly,
in the last sentence, what is 'nice' about the price? Does it look
pleasant when written down? Does it give you a warm glow to
contemplate it? Is it used just because it rhymes with 'price'? If
what you mean is (and it usually is) that the price represents
value for money, then 'competitive' is much more to the point.

If you feel that your own vocabulary lacks range, a useful tool is
a thesaurus. This is a reference book which contains lists of synonyms (or near-synonyms), that is, words with a similar meaning.
If you start with a word or idea, you can look it up and you will
be offered a variety of alternatives to use instead. Looking up a
word in a thesaurus may help you to find a more exact term, a
livelier phrase or a simpler expression to replace something technical or complicated.

One thing to bear in mind, however, is that a thesaurus is not the same thing as a dictionary. Synonyms listed in a thesaurus should not be taken as precise definitions of the word under which they are listed, and there will be subtle distinctions between the words. For this reason, it is always a good idea to use a thesaurus in conjunction with a dictionary.

The more you look for different vocabulary the more you will increase your own stock. If you have difficulty in remembering new words, make a note of them somewhere, whether on paper or in a file on your PC. Of course, if you are writing using a word-processing program you will probably have a thesaurus function available to you. This can be used to find a synonym to replace a word that you have used too often or to find a word that you can't quite call to mind but whose sense you know.

An extensive vocabulary is a possession worth having for its own sake, but in terms of writing, it allows you to vary the words you use, and a varied vocabulary is one of the elements of good writing that helps to keep a reader interested.

One important vocabulary tip for writing reports (or indeed any other piece of serious writing) is: don't use a word if you don't know what it means! It is surprising how often people fall into the trap of hearing a word that impresses them, thinking (mistakenly) that they have grasped its meaning, then going on to use it wrongly, sometimes with ludicrous effect. Use words to impress the reader if you must, but remember that using them wrongly will have the opposite effect. If you are not absolutely sure of a word's meaning, look it up in your dictionary before you commit it to print in your report.

Style

Style refers to the way in which a particular person writes, what it is that distinguishes one writer from another. What we have in common is that we are all writing in English. If we have a good grasp of grammar and a reasonably wide vocabulary then we have access to the same basic range of material. Where differences come in is in the choices we make, such as of words or of sentence structures.

First, you should be aware if there is a house style to be applied in writing your report. This is simply a manual of the rules for the presentation of text that has been adopted by a particular company or other organization. People working for the same employer will come from all sorts of educational backgrounds or even different countries, whether English-speaking or not. They will have their own styles that they will naturally use when writing, and while what they produce may not necessarily be wrong, the different styles may clash with one another. The point of having a house style is to ensure that everyone within the organization who is producing a document is doing so in a standardized way, a way that will be familiar to their colleagues and will present a uniform, identifiable appearance. By following a house style, individuals will be given guidance on such topics as:

- spelling, including whether British or American, whether using -*ise* or -*ize*, etc
- the preferred style of punctuation
- when to use italic or bold type
- when to use capital letters
- the use and presentation of abbreviations

- whether numbers are presented in words or figures
- the level of formality/informality of language

Following a house style removes the need to worry about style decisions, but in the following section we are going to assume that no such house style applies to you and that you therefore need guidance on matters of style.

One of the chief considerations in deciding on style is the target readership, and this is no different in report writing. How will those who commissioned your report expect it to be presented in terms of style? Is it expected to be formal or informal, or somewhere in between?

As we have already seen above, the whole point of a report is to deliver information that can be used as the basis for making necessary decisions. It is not the place for showing off your dazzling literary gifts, daunting the reader with your effortless command of obscure language, or being content to suggest ideas without being so pedestrian as to spell them out. This doesn't mean your writing has to be utterly dry. By all means try to engage and hold the reader's attention as best you can; try to make reading your report a pleasant and informative experience rather than a tedious chore.

On the other hand, you can't treat a report as if it is nothing more than an extended e-mail, or a text message that goes on so long that your thumbs threaten to drop off. You can't use highly informal language or the abbreviations you usually make in texting. Using proper words doesn't equate with exaggerated formality: it is simply a courtesy to the reader to make your writing as understandable as possible. Apart from any other consideration, in the multinational world of modern communications, it may always be the case that your report will be read by someone whose first language is not English. While they may have a working knowledge of business English, they should not be expected to have to puzzle out the meaning of slang or current buzz words.

Try to make your sentences flow in a smooth and logical manner, and do vary your vocabulary (as we have already looked at above), but always bear in mind that it is the message that matters most here, not the way in which it is expressed. The results of your report might be decisive or inconclusive; they may recommend something or nothing; but they must be expressed clearly if they are to be of any value. Let's look at some of the differences between formal and informal styles.

In general terms, in formal report writing you will tend to find long sentences, technical or specialist vocabulary, and a stricter attention to the rules of grammar. You will *not* find much humour or unconventional construction. You will be expected to use what is called the third person impersonal or 'passive voice'.

What this means, essentially, is that instead of writing 'I looked at three different kinds of printer' you would write 'Three different kinds of printer were looked at'; instead of 'I noted that Printer A tended to overheat after extended use' you would write 'It was noted that Printer A tended to overheat after extended use'; instead of 'I didn't think that this mattered' you would write 'This was not considered important', and so on. One great advantage of this style of writing is that it gives an air of impartiality. By not referring to yourself constantly, you are helping to keep the reader's focus on what you are saying, not who is saying it. Not only do you exclude yourself from mention but you also avoid naming other people where this is not required or relevant.

For example, take these two sentences: 'Most people interviewed preferred Printer B' and 'Jane, Derek, Shaheen, Walter and Leslie preferred Printer B, while Yusuf and Brian preferred Printer C'. Not only is the first version more concise and to the point, it also has the advantage of keeping the preferences anonymous. This is more in keeping with the objective and impartial tone required by a formal piece of writing. In addition, it may also be desirable because (a) it is the overall, majority trend that matters rather than each person's individual preference, (b) the people interviewed may prefer not to be identified, and (c) the people reading the report may neither know nor care who these people are.

Don't tie yourself in knots when trying to keep to the passive voice, however. If you find you are faced with the choice between some awkward convoluted construction and actually referring to yourself, you can preserve the formality by describing yourself as 'the writer of this report' or 'the present writer', later reducing this to 'the writer'.

In a formal report you will not be expected to use colloquial contractions:

INFORMAL	FORMAL
I'm	*I am*
you're	*you are*
we're	*we are*
can't	*cannot*
won't	*will not*
isn't	*is not*
shouldn't	*should not*
didn't	*did not*

You will tend to use more formal words rather than their informal equivalents.

STYLE

INFORMAL	FORMAL
get (hold of)	*obtain, achieve, acquire, procure*
check out, look at	*examine, investigate, consider*
go into	*analyse, detail*
get together	*meet*
head-to-head	*meeting, interview*
confab	*conversation, discussion*
pricey	*costly, expensive*
sort out	*arrange, organize*
turn out	*produce, manufacture*
cash	*money, funds*
stuff	*material, equipment*
piece of kit	*piece of equipment, machine, appliance, device, apparatus, tool*
boss	*manager, superior, director, executive, employer, supervisor*
techie	*computer technician*
sack	*dismiss, discharge*
hire	*employ, appoint, recruit*

If you mention individuals by name, give them their formal title and job title (if relevant).

INFORMAL	FORMAL
Jim	*Mr Johnstone/Buying Assistant*
Katie	*Ms Flynn/Personnel Director*

Above all, be consistent. If you introduce the person by their formal name/*title*, keep it that way throughout. Don't refer to 'Mr Johnstone' on one page and 'Jim' somewhere else.

Plain English

In the mid-1970s a campaign began in Britain to eliminate 'gob-bledegook' from public writing and replace this with Plain English – simple, direct English that was free from jargon (see below for a discussion of this) and easy for ordinary members of the public to understand. This campaign continues today and many of its principles have been adopted by public and private organizations.

As far as report writing is concerned, it is obvious that the goal must be to make what you want to say completely accessible to everyone who might read it (without oversimplifying). The following are ways in which you can make your English clear and understandable:

- Keep your vocabulary as simple as possible, leaving out any words that are too obscure, excessively formal or old-fashioned. If, as may well often happen, technical terms are unavoidable, explain them where you first use them or define them in a glossary.
- Cut out any words or phrases that are simply padding and don't add anything to the meaning.
- Resist the temptation to show off your writing skills to try to impress your readers: report writing is not entertainment but a means of communicating information.
- Keep your sentences short and to the point. Aim at fitting the content of your sentence into between 15 and 30 words.
- Similarly, try to avoid very long paragraphs: you can usually split them after four or five sentences.

Jargon

Jargon is essentially the kind of informal language that is used within a particular profession or group. It consists of words and phrases that are not necessarily part of the standard terminology of a subject, but are used to communicate information quickly and easily between members of the group. Jargon may contain informal expressions for more long-winded technical terms, and it may also involve alternatives for everyday words. It is not the same as technical language, which in many cases represents the only way of referring to specialist items. In any case, technical terms should be explained when you use them or defined in a glossary.

When people who are familiar with the intricacies and fine distinctions to be made in a particular field get together, they often slip into jargon. Apart from anything else, use of this kind of language can help individuals feel that they are a part of a community, that they are insiders. Some people use jargon simply because it makes what they say seem more impressive or that a fancy word sounds better than a plain one; others because they think these expressions represent the only possible way of saying it. For the general reader, however, much of this will be meaningless.

The world of business is particularly prone to jargonizing, and it is all too easy to reach for the ready-made phrase or word automatically instead of really thinking about what you want to say. The effect of this can be, at best, to make your meaning unnecessarily obscure, or, at worst, lead you into saying or writing things that really have little meaning at all. Consider the following example.

> *We are planning to bring a new initiative on stream to build on our existing methodology for continuous quality improvement and package best practices and innovations into an effective knowledge management system.*

Some might find this impressive, might feel it hits all the right buttons or demonstrates a good grasp of up-to-date vocabulary.

Others, however, will simply squirm in horror. It is the second part of the population that you should have in mind when writing your report: the last thing you want is for your report to induce squirming in influential readers. How could this example have been better put? It could have read something like this:

> *We are planning to introduce a new idea that will be an improvement on what is already an excellent system.*

This is the essence of the first version but without the fancy stuff that really doesn't add any meaning. Which would you prefer to read? In the following table you will find a few examples of jargon terms. If you want to keep your report free of jargon, try to avoid them and consider using the alternatives suggested.

JARGON	ALTERNATIVE
axiomatic	*assumed, obvious*
ballpark figure	*(rough) estimate, best guess*
best practice	*what works best*
challenging	*difficult*
cut to the chase	*come to the point*
cutting-edge	*advanced, breaking new ground, innovative*
deliver	*provide, supply, carry out*
dynamic	*active, energetic*
facility	*means, opportunity*
game plan	*plan of action, strategy*
head up	*lead, be in charge of*

in the current climate	at the moment, as things stand, now, currently
in the pipeline	on the way, coming, about to happen
inaugurate	start, introduce
initiative	scheme, project
interface	to connect, to work with
interpersonal skills	ability to get on with other people
joined-up	coherent, co-ordinated
key	important, essential
meaningful	valid, useful, worthwhile
nominate	choose, select
ongoing	continuing, existing, in progress
on-stream	in operation, in use
package	to put together, unite
parameter	boundary, limit
within the parameters	within the scope
proactive	taking the initiative, initiating action, creative, energetic
quality-driven	with quality as a priority
remit	responsibility
roll out	introduce, bring in, phase in
scenario	series of events, plan, situation

situation	This can often be dropped altogether. A 'crisis situation' is merely a 'crisis'; a 'panic situation' is the same as a 'panic', and so on.
state-of-the-art	best available, best of its kind, newest, first-class
syndrome	pattern
synergy	co-operation, working together, co-ordinated action
take on board	accept, recognize, take into account
track record	history, past performance, experience
user-friendly	easy to use, straightforward
workshop	meeting, discussion

Slang

One of the tricks of the writing business, no matter in which particular area of it you are involved, is to know which words belong in which places. There are some words and phrases that, although they may be widely used in all sorts of circumstances, are best avoided when you are writing a report. Many of these fall under the heading of slang.

Slang exists on the borders of Standard English. It often originates from groups of people who are outside the mainstream of society or see themselves as different in some way. It is associated with, among others, young people, rock musicians, rappers, computer hackers, skateboarding enthusiasts and drug users. By its nature, slang tends to be very much of its time and can very

135

quickly become dated. Many regions and trades also have their own forms of slang.

A good dictionary will indicate if a word is considered to be slang; if you have any doubts about whether or not a word is suitable for use in your report, you can always look it up to make sure.

Although many slang words are widely understood (such as *gob* for 'mouth', *fag* for 'cigarette' or *dosh* for 'money') these will produce a highly informal style when used in writing. Using words like these in a formal report would give your readers the impression that you simply did not appreciate what sort of language the situation required. This might lead them to have doubts about the content of your report as well as the language it was written in.

For example, in your report you might wish to refer to comments made by people you have interviewed or who have filled in questionnaires. What they actually said might run along these lines:

> *Paula from Purchasing said the new printer was wicked.*
>
> *'Way cool,' was my mate Jack's reaction.*
>
> *Charmaine said she didn't want to diss it, but it wasn't all that.*

This kind of language is both vivid and to the point. It would be perfectly appropriate in conversation, but in a formal report you would have to think about recasting the content:

> *Two out of three colleagues described the printer as excellent. A third found it to be satisfactory but not the best available.*

It is a good idea to be aware of slang words that you habitually use, and be on your guard against letting any of them slip into your report writing.

Sensitive language

Another type of language to keep out of your report is the kind that some of your readers might find offensive. You might think that this is political correctness gone crazy or that nobody is going to run away with the idea that you have deliberately tried to offend them. However, you have to bear in mind continually that you want your report to be read and that you want people to pay attention to what you write. Don't take the chance of putting anybody off if you can help it.

Even apparently innocent language can have unwanted effects if it is used insensitively. Language can reinforce unhelpful stereotypes, promote negative opinions and patronize people. On the other hand, sensitive use of language can have effects that are opposite to these, helping to break down stereotypes and promote positive images.

The following are the main areas where sensitive language is required:

- gender
- race and nationality
- religion
- physical and mental capability

In addition to these, you should apply the general principles (see below) of sensitive language when dealing with the subjects of:

- age
- sexuality

- marital or family status
- political beliefs

Sensitive use of language is a complicated and emotive area. There are no fixed rules about what is acceptable and what is inappropriate, and people often disagree. However, you may find the following general principles helpful:

- Some traditional ways of referring to people may reinforce ideas that are unhelpful and often incorrect, for example with regard to the roles of men and women within society or the lifestyles and values of minority ethnic groups.
- On the other hand, well-intentioned attempts to avoid insensitive language can sometimes interfere with the clear or direct expression of meaning, and can appear ridiculous if taken to extremes.
- People usually prefer to be regarded as individuals rather than as members of a particular group, and often it is simply not relevant to refer to their race, gender or physical capability.
- There are often differences between the ways people refer to themselves, and the ways in which they prefer others to refer to them. It is a good idea to respect such differences, and bear in mind that a group may use a term freely but object to its use by people outside the group.
- Ideas about what is appropriate might vary from country to country or region to region. They can also change over time, with the result that terms that were at one time considered unobjectionable might now be taken as being offensive.

Gender

You risk offending many of your readers if you use language in a way that implies that there is only one gender, or that one gender is superior to the other. It probably goes without saying that you should avoid crude generalizations based on stereotypical portrayals of men and women. However, the subject of gender also poses some more subtle problems for writers.

Using words in ways that reinforce stereotypes about the roles that men and women play in society is something that is easily done, and most of us will have done it at one time or another without thinking too deeply about it. This can happen when language reflects ideas about gender roles that are now regarded as being old-fashioned. If you want to avoid perpetuating gender stereotypes, here are a few suggestions:

- When talking about a person's occupation, use neutral terms rather than gender-specific ones. For example, you could say *chair* or *chairperson* rather than chairman; *spokesperson* rather than spokesman.
- Avoid using titles that imply that an occupation is done by only one gender:

GENDER-SPECIFIC NAME	PREFERRED TERM
dustman	*refuse collector*
fireman	*firefighter*
foreman	*supervisor*
salesman	*sales representative*
taxman	*tax collector*

- Avoid using words ending in *-ess* when referring to a woman's occupation, especially when there is a neutral alternative available. Many of these words (such as *manageress* or *directress*) can be taken as suggesting that there is something unusual about a woman holding a particular role.
- Bear in mind that some readers may object to the word *man* being used to refer to both men and women in phrases like *the benefits that science has brought to modern man*. A moment's thought may provide you with a suitable alternative:

GENDER-SPECIFIC NAME	PREFERRED TERM
man	*people, humanity, the human race, humankind*
man-hours	*working hours*
mankind	*humankind, humanity, the human race*
man-made	*artificial, synthetic*

Beware of traditional grammatical constructions that treat the masculine gender as the normal or natural form, or imply that it can be used to include both genders. Many people object to the use of masculine pronouns (*he*, *his* or *him*) in sentences that refer equally to men and women, as in:

> *Every applicant should include his curriculum vitae.*
>
> *Anyone can use this printer if he is familiar with the previous model.*

Some people prefer to use the plural words *they*, *their* and *them* (which are conveniently sexless) in such situations. Some purists maintain that this kind of usage is not grammatical, but it is now very common and most people will not object to it:

> *Every applicant should include their curriculum vitae.*
>
> *Anyone can use this printer if they are familiar with the previous model.*

Other people prefer to use *he or she*, *his or hers* and *him or her*, but this can begin to look rather clumsy or heavy-handed when these phrases have to be repeated frequently:

Every applicant should include his or her curriculum vitae.

Anyone can use this printer if he or she is familiar with the previous model.

Perhaps the best solution is to rewrite the sentence in a way that avoids this sort of problem altogether, such as by using *a* instead of a pronoun, or by rephrasing:

Every applicant should include a curriculum vitae.

Anyone who is familiar with the previous model can use this printer.

The problem can also be avoided by making the subject of the sentence plural:

All applicants should include their curriculum vitae.

Everybody can use this printer if they are familiar with the previous model.

Race and nationality

The subject of race and nationality is another area that requires sensitive treatment. Again, it is not just a question of avoiding crude stereotypes and deliberately offensive terms. Sensitive use of language should also involve:

- being aware of appropriate terms to refer to people's race or racial origin. For example, *Afro-Caribbean* is often thought to be preferable to *West Indian*, and *British Asian* (rather than *Indian*, *Pakistani* or *Bangladeshi*) is often preferred for British citizens whose families originate from the Indian subcontinent;

- using positive terms rather than defining people by what they are not. Terms such as *non-white* should only be used when the context makes them relevant;
- taking care to use terms relating to race and nationality accurately. Inaccurate use of such terms can give the impression that you don't care enough about whom you are writing or who will be reading it to observe correct distinctions. For example, people who are Scottish, Welsh or Irish will probably not be impressed if you use *English* when you are actually referring to the whole population of the British Isles.

Certain inaccurate uses of terms relating to race are particularly likely to cause offence:

- *Immigrants* are people of a different nationality who have come to a foreign country to settle in it; the term does not apply to people who were born in that country but happen to be of a different racial group from the majority of the population.
- *Black* does not refer to everyone who is not white.
- *Ethnic minorities* are not necessarily equivalent to non-whites. In many parts of the world white people are an ethnic minority.

Religion

Most of the points mentioned above referring to race and nationality also hold true when referring to religion. In addition you should be aware of the following:

- Religions (such as *Islam*, *Judaism*, *Christianity*) are usually spelled with a capital letter, as are religious denominations (such as *Protestant*, *Catholic*, *Sunni*, *Shia*), religious festivals (such as *Easter*, *Ramadan*, *Diwali, Passover*) and religious texts (such as *the Bible*, *the Upanishads*).

- Most Muslims prefer the spellings *Makkah* and *Quran* to *Mecca* and *Koran* when referring respectively to the holy city and the sacred book of Islam.

- Avoid assuming that all members of a particular racial group share the same religion. For example, not all Asians are Muslims.

Physical and mental capability

Some of the language traditionally used when referring to people with disabilities has associations of passivity, limitation and pity. It often causes disabled people to be seen in terms of their disability rather than as individual human beings with their own characters and personal concerns. There are a number of things you can do to avoid this:

- Beware of describing people solely in terms of a disability, as though that defined their personality. Don't use terms like *cripple* or *invalid*: use instead *a person with a disability* or *a disabled person*. Similarly, it is preferable to talk about *people with epilepsy* rather than *epileptics*, *vision-impaired people* rather than the *blind*.

- Many disabled people dislike being referred to as *handicapped* on the grounds that a handicap is created by external surroundings or other people's attitudes (for example a building without a lift for a wheelchair user, or discrimination in the workplace) and not by the disability itself.

- Avoid inaccurate or outdated language. Where a recognized medical term exists, such as *cerebral palsy* or *Down's syndrome*, it is advisable to use it.

- Although the word *challenged* is common (particularly in North America) as part of compounds that refer to disabilities (for example, *visually challenged* to mean *blind* or *partially sighted*), this is often avoided in British English because it has lent itself to a way of making fun of the idea of political correctness (as in the use of *vertically challenged* to mean *short*). The terms *differently abled* and *special* can also attract ridicule for the same reason.

Clichés

A lot of phrases that start out as fashionable and new or as examples of jargon end up as a cliché. What this means is any expression that has been used so often that it has lost any freshness it once had. It is better to try to avoid clichés. For one thing, using too many of them will give your readers the impression that you haven't given a lot of thought to what you want to say; for another, they may decide that you don't have anything original to contribute and are merely recycling hackneyed ideas. There are various types of clichés.

Some similes have been used so often that they have become clichés:

> *as bright as a button*
> *as bold as brass*
> *drink like a fish*

Some metaphors have been used so often that they have become clichés:

> *a baptism of fire*
> *take the bull by the horns*
> *hell on wheels*

Some quotations and proverbs have been used so often that they have become clichés:

> *beggars can't be choosers*

> *all work and no play ...*
> *the blind leading the blind*

Some idiomatic turns of phrase have been used so often that they have become clichés:

> *add insult to injury*
> *at the end of the day*
> *last but not least*

Some adjectives have been used so often with certain nouns that they have become clichés. In cases like these, the adjective becomes devalued and adds little or nothing to the meaning. Omit it altogether if you can't think of a more original or apt alternative:

> *a burning question*
> *a gaping hole*
> *a glowing tribute*
> *a graphic description*
> *fulsome praise*
> *the vast majority*

Expressions become clichés because they originally had a certain appeal: perhaps the particular series of words sounded well together, or perhaps they simply summed up a situation neatly. When you add the ease of familiarity to the mix you can see why they are often an automatic choice for the lazy writer. If you don't want to come across as unoriginal or lazy, weed those clichés out!

Avoiding waffle

In report writing, as in most forms of writing, it is important to avoid the tendency to waffle. Essentially, waffling is going on and on about something in a repetitive and increasingly irrelevant way. Some people who are guilty of this are simply trying to fill up a set amount of space or fulfil a target number of words when they have run out of pertinent things to say. Other writers may not be aware that they are doing it, having lost concentration or forgotten that they have already covered a particular point. In any case, no one is going to want to read this sort of thing:

> It has been drawn to our attention that certain persons unknown have being seeing fit to avail themselves illegally of the various papers, envelopes, address labels and stationery supplies provided for the use of the administrative assistants only. At this point in time it is absolutely key to make the point once and for all that all necessary measures will be taken to totally eradicate and literally stamp out this most deplorable and indefensible practice. A comprehensive menu of strict disciplinary measures, from verbal warnings for first offences, ratcheting up to suspension or eventual dismissal, is currently being made available to senior staff, and these will be undertaken if any culprits are detected in the act or otherwise identified. These measures will come into force with immediate effect as of next Monday morning at 8.30am sharp.

What's wrong with this? Where to begin? First of all, it is pompous, reeking of a self-satisfied and self-important attitude. It goes out of its way to use big, fancy, official-sounding words rather than direct ones. Also, it is unnecessarily repetitive.

WAFFLE	ALTERNATIVE
and also	and
apart from the fact that	except for
as a consequence of	because of
as a matter of fact	in fact
as to whether	whether
at this moment in time	now
be of the opinion	believe, think
because of the fact that	because
by virtue of the fact that	because
due to the fact that	because
during the course of	during
in a majority of cases	mostly, usually
in a very real sense	You could substitute something like *truly*, but in fact this phrase could be dropped altogether with no loss.
in all probability	probably
in point of fact	in fact
in spite of the fact that	although
in the event of	if

in the neighbourhood of	about, approximately
in this day and age	now
irrespective of the fact that	although
not to put too fine a point on it	to speak plainly
on a daily basis	daily, every day
prior to	before
subsequent to	after
the reason is because	because
to all intents and purposes	essentially, practically
with a view to	to
with the exception of	except

It contains at least two erroneous uses of words. 'Illegal' means against the law, while what is meant here is 'against the rules or regulations' of the organization. The police aren't going to come looking for someone who used an envelope they weren't entitled to. Also, it is a common mistake to think that 'literally' is a word you can use just to intensify the next word or phrase, like 'utterly', for example. If you literally do something, this means that you do it in reality. It seems unlikely that anyone in this case will find heavy boots stamping on their sticky fingers.

It is not difficult to cut through this sort of stuff and emphasize what's really important. Simply think about what it is that has to be said, then say it as clearly and directly as possible. For example, without losing anything of value, the passage above could be reduced to something like the following:

> *Too much unauthorized use of stationery is going on.*
> *From now on, anyone caught doing this will find them-*
> *selves in serious trouble.*

Of course, this is an exaggerated example, but it gets the point across. To help you take up the slack in your writing, here is a list of waffle expressions and suggested alternatives that are clearer and more to the point.

Another form of redundancy in writing is tautology. What this means is repeating something that is already implied in what has already been said. For example, *in actual fact* is tautological because facts are necessarily actual, or else they wouldn't be facts in the first place! Similarly, the 'past' in *past history* is unnecessary: it is only history if it is in the past.

What's so bad about that? Most people use tautology in every-day speech and idiomatic writing. However, some of those who read your report might be sticklers for proper use of language and as such may be put off by this kind of linguistic redundancy. You want your readers to concentrate on what you are saying and avoid distracting them by the way you say it. Here are a few examples of tautology in which the element in italics can be omitted without losing any of the meaning:

absolutely unique	meet *with*
added extra	*new* innovation
collaborate *together*	*quite* unique
consensus *of opinion*	refer *back*
early beginnings	revert *back*
end result	sufficient *enough*
free gift	*unexpected* surprise
future prospects	*utterly* unique
link *together*	

AVOIDING WAFFLE

Here are a few simple tips to remember if you want to avoid waffle:

- Try not to use several words where one would do.
- Get into the habit of pruning words and phrases that do not actively add anything to the meaning.
- Don't waste time and space telling your readers things they already know.

Consistency

In any piece of professional writing it is important to be consistent. This will involve making decisions about how you are going to present information and making sure that you stick to these decisions throughout the document. If your writing is consistent, your readers will know where they stand and it will be easier for them to follow your message.

Consistency can take a number of forms:

- Be consistent in reference. Take care to present information in a consistent way throughout your report. Where there is a choice between ways of presenting something, decide which is more suitable and stick to it. This gives your readers the feeling that you are in command of your material and how you want them to perceive it.

- Be consistent in argument. Maintain the same approach to your subject throughout your report. You may be aware of different points of view or different sides to a discussion, but once you have chosen to present a particular viewpoint don't waver or change your mind part of the way through. If you do, your readers will become confused or feel that you didn't think the report through thoroughly enough before you started writing. If you come across as undecided or unconvinced you are hardly likely to convince anybody else.

- Be consistent in tone. The way you write will tend to reveal the way you think about your subject. For example, you may write in a detached way, an enthusiastic way or a sceptical way. Whatever tone you decide to adopt, be sure to use it throughout the report.

- Be consistent in register. Think about the readers of your report and what style of English they will prefer. Whether you choose formal or informal language, you must stick to your choice throughout the report.

There should be a single personality behind your writing, and being consistent helps your readers to become familiar with that personality.

Illustrative material

Especially in longer reports, it can often be a good idea to augment your text with tables, diagrams, graphs, charts or other illustrations. Long, unbroken chunks of text can present a chore for even the keenest reader and great wodges of percentages and statistics can be hard to digest.

Purely factual information can often benefit from being presented in the form of lists, tables or diagrams. A well-designed and clear table or diagram can be easier for a reader to understand than a lengthy verbal description. Here are a few suggested guidelines for dealing with this kind of material.

- Make sure that your illustrations are placed as close as possible to the part of the text that they illustrate. Readers will find it irritating to have to hunt for something that should be immediately obvious. If, however, this is not practicable (for example, your illustrations might be too big or too numerous to appear without seriously disrupting the flow of the report) it might be a better idea to gather all illustrations in an appendix at the end of the document.

- Give each item a number, followed by a title. Some writers or house styles will refer to all examples of graphic material as *Figures*. Others, however, make distinctions between illustrations and tables. If you are using the latter style, each type of illustration should be categorized by a separate numbering sequence. In this way, if, for example, you wanted to display two drawings or diagrams and a table, you would label them as *Figure 1*, *Figure 2* (sometimes abbreviated to *Fig. 1*, *Fig. 2*, etc) and *Table 1*.

- Make sure that each title is clear and informative so that the reader can make sense of the illustration or table without having to look anywhere else. Place the number and title at the bottom of an illustration, but at the top of a table. Remember to include a scale for each graph or chart if necessary. A good rule of thumb is to opt for the most simple form of illustration; these tend to be the clearest to read.

- Do not repeat data in the text that you have already supplied in a table. Instead, refer in the body of the text to the illustration or table by its number: *see Table 2* or *Figure (ii) shows that ...*

Some word-processing programs have the facility to create and insert a table. Here is an example of the kind of table you can create. It is up to you to decide on the styles and sizes of type to use.

Table 1a: Holiday entitlement of employees in reprographics department, 2007.

Employee	Years of service	Holiday entitlement (days)
A.B.	10	30
C.D.	8	24
E.F.	1	20
G.H.	6	22
I.J.	7	23

Other forms of illustrative material include graphs, flow charts, bar charts and pie charts. Unlike tables, you will not be able to create these using your word processor (unless you are using specialist software). Depending on your budget, you may be able to have these professionally produced, either within or outside your organization, or you may simply have to draw them yourself and scan them into your report.

A **graph** consists of two axes at right angles to one another and marked off in measurements, on which a number of values are plotted as dots which are then joined by a line. Graphs are most useful for showing trends over a period or time, or the way in which two or more variables are related.

A **flow chart** is essentially a pictorial representation of a process of some kind, usually constructed of boxes containing individual steps in that process, connected by arrows showing their relative positions or stages.

A **bar chart** is a type of graph, with two axes but showing quantities by means of vertical rectangular blocks (or bars). It is a vivid way of presenting statistical information, allowing the reader to see the range and variation of values clearly and quickly, rather than having to analyse bare statistics.

A pie chart takes the form of a circle divided into sections by radii so as to show relative numbers or quantities. Each quantity shown looks like a slice of a pie (hence the name) and this is a quick way of grasping the proportion of the whole that each represents.

Desktop publishing, using, for example, scanners and software for sourcing and manipulating photographic material, makes incorporating photos and artwork into your report that much easier. If you do not have these facilities, you may be faced with the choice of paying to have this done or omitting this kind of illustration altogether. Ask yourself if the illustrations are really necessary, or do they simply represent a fancy, but dispensable, extra feature.

Revision

Once you have finished a single complete version of your report, you then have the opportunity to change and improve it. No one can be expected to come up with a perfect piece of work at the first attempt. It is usually more helpful to produce something that is complete but imperfect and then revise and rework it, rather than waste your time trying to produce from scratch something that will be so perfectly honed that no further work is required.

You might think that what you have produced is a pretty good piece of work; maybe it is, but you still need to read it over again with a critical eye. Check that all of the key points that you wanted to deal with have been covered in a logical order, and that everything you have included actually contributes something to the report as a whole.

Check also that you deal with each issue clearly and that you move smoothly from one point to the next. If you find that this isn't the case, add more material to explain, introduce, link or summarize where necessary, as this will make your work more polished.

Once you are satisfied with the overall structure and content, you can concentrate on getting the introduction and the conclusion right. You may find that what you said originally in your introduction is no longer completely accurate because of changes that you have made during the writing process itself. Now is the time to look at this again and tailor it to the actual final content of your report.

If you are happy that your report is well organized and coherent as a whole, you can turn your attention to the details. Make sure your writing is:

- **correct**, so that there are no errors in facts, spelling, grammar, punctuation, appropriate style and use of language.
- **consistent**, so that things are expressed in the same way each time you refer to them, and you have followed the same style and the same layout throughout.
- **clear**, so that the language used is easy to read, information is easy to understand, and text is attractively laid out, with plenty of space and enough headings to help your readers, but not so many that they interrupt the flow of the report.
- **complete**, so that all of the relevant material is in place, including explanations of unfamiliar terms and abbreviations, any background information and acknowledgement of your sources.
- **concise**, so that the language and the amount and level of information are presented in the simplest and most direct way possible.

Once you have completed your revisions and reworkings, print out your report. When you have done this and are holding the document in your hands, you need to look over it again to make sure that everything is in order before you hand it over or send it off to the person or people who will read it. At this stage you might be forgiven for thinking that you've done enough; you might even be sick of the sight of your own work and just want to get the whole thing over with!

It is often a good idea to put it aside for a couple of days while you work on something else. Sometimes when you have been working hard on a project you can become too close to it and find yourself unable to look at it objectively. Put a little distance between yourself and your report. When you come back to it you will be able to look at it afresh, assess it clear-sightedly and spot any mistakes or areas that could stand a little improvement.

Above all, don't take this stage lightly; it is a vital part of the report-writing process. This is not the time to skim over your work. Everything needs to be in good order so that you can get your message across effectively to your reader(s). You need to be sure of creating a favourable impression so that your finished report attracts comments for the right reasons rather than the wrong ones. They say no news is good news: it is better if your work attracts no comments at all, because there is nothing to find fault with, rather than the other alternative.

Although you may well have been looking at what you have written for some time on a computer screen, it needs to be checked on paper as well to make sure that it looks and reads just as you want it to. The way a piece of writing looks on a computer monitor and the way it looks when printed out on paper are not always as similar as you might expect.

Documents can acquire a whole new identity when the density of the ink, the sharpness of the printing, the texture, brilliance and thickness of the paper, and the varying light conditions of the real world come into play. Fonts, sizes of type, headings, spaces and blocks of text all may look different when you are holding a piece of paper in your hands rather than staring at the screen.

This is something we will look at again in more detail under 'Presentation' on pages 164–74, but for now you can get a feel of what we're talking about here by holding your report at arm's length and staring hard at it. Try deliberately blurring your vision (If you wear glasses, simply take them off for a moment!), so that all you get is a visual impression rather than being able to read what the words actually say. Your computer may be able to offer you a 'full page view' that gives a similar effect to this, but there is no substitute for physically doing this in reality.

When all you see is black marks on a white surface, you will be better placed to decide whether or not those black marks are truly well arranged, rather than be distracted by automatically thinking about what they mean. It may even be a good idea to print early versions of your report just to get an approximate idea of the way it will look. This will allow you to spot any alterations that should be made to the layout before you have gone so far that reshaping the whole thing will be an enormous chore that you would rather not face.

To check for consistency of layout, try holding the document at arm's length (You can put your glasses back on now!) and flicking through it. Again, this will give you an immediate impression of what things look like rather than what they say.

Proofreading

This is something you might not have had to do before, although some people do it for a living. Essentially proofreading is looking at text to identify and correct errors. At this stage you should not be thinking about whether the information is factually accurate or clearly expressed. There is no judgment to be made here on the quality of the writing; by the time this stage is reached, it is assumed that the text is going to be printed. Rather, the sole intention is to carefully check spelling, punctuation and grammar, and alphabetical and numerical order. In fact, professional proofreaders might even read a book backwards so that all they see is a succession of words rather than a coherent text. You'll be glad to know that we don't go so far as to recommend doing this with your report!

REVISION

Successful proofreaders tend not to assume that a document will be correct, and focus actively on looking for mistakes. Proofreading therefore requires you to be more alert and critical than usual, and to keep this up for quite a long period of time. Because this level of concentration can be difficult to maintain, sometimes people experience a kind of 'word blindness' when trying to proofread. This is especially true when they are looking at their own work. Because they are so familiar with it, and know exactly what they mean to say, they tend to picture it in the way they expect it to read, rather than the way it actually appears in black and white on the page.

To overcome the problems that can be associated with proofreading your own work, it is usually a good idea to ask someone else to proofread it. A fresh pair of eyes will often immediately spot things that you will miss again and again.

However, the ultimate responsibility rests with you, and you should always read through your report yourself as well.

Proofreading tips

It is important to remember that you are actively looking for mistakes in the way your report is written rather than passively absorbing information from the text. Don't get swept away by your peerless prose and rush forward to revel in the truth and beauty of your conclusions! Here are a few things you must remain aware of:

- words that you find difficult to spell: it is a good idea to keep a list of these so that you can look out for your own particular bugbears
- easily confused words, such as *adverse/averse*, *affect/effect*, *ambiguous/ambivalent*, *biannual/biennial*, *comparable/comparative*, *complement/compliment*, *continual/continuous*,

council/counsel, derisive/derisory, discreet/discrete, econo-
mic/economical, fewer/less, incredible/incredulous, lay/lie,
mitigate/militate, passed/past, practicable/practical, prin-
ciple/principal, stationary/stationery, there/their/they're

- the sequence of any numerical ordering, as in paragraphs,
  identification of diagrams and tables, etc
- the sequence of any alphabetic ordering
- the numbering of the pages
- the relevance of running titles on each page, if any
- consistency in the way that words with optional spellings are
  written
- consistency in the way that punctuation marks are used

To make things easy for yourself, it is worth keeping a list of your
'policy decisions' on matters of style and layout, as well as noting down decisions you make about optional spellings, unless
you are following a house style. For example, if you decide to
spell words such as *specialize* with *-ize* rather than *-ise*, make a
note of this and make sure that you apply your chosen policy consistently throughout your report.

A good way of checking the consistency of spellings in your
report is to use the 'Find' function on a word processor. This will
allow you to check whether the document contains any spellings
that you have decided not to use. For example, you might search
for the word *specialise* wherever it occurs, or you might search for
the sequence of letters *ise* and check in each case whether or not
you need to change the spelling to *ize*.

Don't forget to check over any diagrams, tables or illustrations.
Make sure that they are all correctly and accurately captioned
and appearing in the right places. Particularly with tables or
other numerical illustrative material, check that the numbers are
correct. For example, if you are using a pie chart in which each
segment is allotted a percentage, add up the segments to make

sure that the total is 100%. Make sure that any sum you show actually works out as you claim it does. Don't give any reader the opportunity to dismiss your report, after all your hard work, because they can see at a glance that your figures don't add up.

Presentation

Your finished report may consist of no more than a single sheet, or of two sheets stapled together, printed from your own PC and photocopied; on the other hand, it may run to a hundred pages or more. Especially in the latter case, when the writing and typesetting is finished, you have to give some thought to the idea of how your report will appear as a physical document.

No matter how long or short your report is expected to be, it is a mistake to neglect the look of it. Remember that your report is no longer just a collection of words but an object: the appearance, size and feel of it are important. You have to imagine the effect that the act of handling and reading it will have on the reader. Obviously, you would rather that it made a good impression, and that people will be encouraged to read it. The last thing you want is for it to present such a shoddy or cheap appearance that people will assume that the content is equally worthless.

In this section we will look at such practical aspects of the creation of a report as desktop publishing, typography, layout, paper and binding methods.

Desktop publishing

This is the facility to create documents of a publishable standard on an ordinary desktop computer. A desktop publishing package incorporates word processing and graphics applications and will allow you to take decisions on such aspects of a document as typesetting, design, layout and illustration. If you are using desktop publishing you will not only be able to create your report yourself but produce a final version that can be printed.

Typography

In the age of computers, e-mail and text messaging, the most basic form of writing, that of using a pen and paper, is becoming less and less common. One of its undoubted drawbacks is that it allows you only very few forms of presentation that you can use for emphasis. You can underline words or phrases, or you can use capital letters, but that is about it. However, when you are using a computer there is quite a range of devices available to you. When you create a document using a word-processing program, you can change the look of it and help get your point across by considering:

- size of type
- typefaces
- fonts
- page layout

Size of type

The larger the size of type you use, the more you draw the reader's attention to the information that it is expressing. Very large type is used mostly for posters and newspaper headlines, whereas legal and financial agreements are notorious for using small print that discourages the reader from examining particular information too closely.

You should think not only about what size of type you want to use for the main part of your report, but also about whether it is appropriate to use different sizes of type for different parts of the document. For example, you may decide to use a larger size of type for headings, or a smaller size of type for footnotes or captions to graphic material.

PRESENTATION

Have a look at documents that strike you as being attractive to read and well laid out, and see how different type sizes have been used. This is largely a matter of choice and taste, but at least for the most basic of documents, a common size for the bulk of the text is 12 point. Some material may be set a little smaller, in 10 point for example, but it is asking quite a lot of the reader to deal with large amounts of text in a size any smaller than that.

Main headings should be at least 2 points larger than the text size, but you may want to make them even larger if you plan to have subheadings as well. For example, if you have a text size of 12 point, you could make your main headings 16 point, thus allowing you to have a subheading size of 14 point. If you have sub-subheadings (and you may be surprised at how sections of your report seem to demand more and more subdivision!) you can always differentiate these by using different typefaces.

Typefaces

Computers allow you to create text not only in the normal, standard form (known technically as 'roman'), but also using **bold**, <u>underlined</u> and *italic* typefaces. You can use these options to make important words in the text stand out.

Italic type is the most commonly used way of showing emphasis in normal type. It is also traditionally used to indicate certain special types of information, such as foreign words and phrases, titles of books, films, pieces of music or other works of art, and titles of ships or other craft:

We both ordered the *filet mignon*.
The Lord of the Rings was written by J.R.R. Tolkien and made into a trilogy of films by Peter Jackson.
She was one of the crew of the space shuttle *Atlantis*.

Bold type is generally used for headings and letterheads. It can also be used to emphasize individual words and phrases within the body of the text:

> Visitors will **not** be allowed to park in undesignated spaces. The key elements of the strategy are **timing**, **positioning** and **back-up**.

If you have a stretch of text that is already in italics, bold type can be used for emphasis within it.

> *October was originally the **eighth** month.*

Underlined text is used less frequently in word-processed documents. However, it can be used in the same way as bold type to emphasize a word or phrase within a stretch of italic type.

> *October was originally the <u>eighth</u> month.*

If you are using a typewriter rather than a computer, you do not have the option of bold or italic typefaces, so underlined text is used instead of these for emphasis or to indicate special types of information.

Fonts

A font is a particular variety of type, with its own design and basic shape. Some people get confused between a typeface and a font, but the simplest way to remember which is which is to bear in mind that a font can have different typefaces, but not vice versa. Word processors and desktop publishing packages will offer you a wide array of different fonts. Changing the font you use can give a document a very different look and create a markedly different effect on the reader. Here are a few examples of different fonts:

Book Antiqua   Georgia   Courier New

Arial   Verdana

Fonts can be divided into serif fonts and sans serif fonts. In the list shown above, Book Antiqua, Georgia and Courier New are serif fonts: what this means is that they feature small projections called 'serifs' at the ends of the letters. Fonts that have serifs are usually easier to read, the theory being that these small projections help guide the eye from one letter to the next, and it is preferable to use this sort of font for longer documents.

Fonts that do not have serifs, such as Arial and Verdana, are known as sans serif fonts. These types of fonts are often considered to be cleaner and more modern-looking than serif fonts. They can create a striking impression, but they are usually best avoided for longer documents.

In choosing a font, you have to think about the impression you wish to create and the overall appearance of your report. A comparatively short and informal report will come across perfectly well in a sans serif font, even lending it a more personal air. A longer and more formal report will usually require the more serious tone given by the use of a serif font.

Whichever font you choose, it is important to stick to it throughout the document. Use of too many fonts will give it a bitty, unfinished look. In the same way, use either bold or underlined headings, but not both.

Page layout

Word-processing programs allow you to customize the layout of your page to create the effect that you prefer. You should think about how you can use the following features to create a look that is both attractive to the reader and in keeping with the message that you are interested in communicating:

- What size and typeface do you want to use for headings? Headings need to be large enough to stand out from the surrounding text. You may choose to use different styles for different levels of heading to show that some are more important than others.

- What width of margins do you want to use? If you use wider margins, this will create a narrower column of text and mean that fewer words will fit onto each line.

- Do you want the text to be 'justified' (so that each line is the same length and the margins are straight)? Having straight margins tends to give a more formal, authoritative look to a document, whereas a 'ragged' right-hand margin can make it appear more informal and accessible.

- Are you planning to indent your paragraphs (with the exception of those opening a chapter or section), or would you prefer to insert space between them?

- Do you want the text to have single or double spaces between the lines? A double-spaced text will give more room for readers to write comments on, and this may be a desirable feature for many readers of your report.

- Do you want to use different colours? Desktop publishing packages will allow you to use different colours of ink for your text. This can be useful in emphasizing particular words or phrases, or in differentiating one block of text from another. However, in a serious formal report too much use of different colours may look out of place and give readers the impression that they are not being offered a serious piece of work.

- Do you want to use graphical features such as borders, tables and bullet points to highlight certain types of information?

Layout of reports

Because reports can be long documents with many different sections and detailed information, it is important that your report is physically presented in a clear and attractive way.

- Use plenty of headings and subheadings. These will help your reader to focus on the important points and guide them through the report. Also, a page that is broken up by headings presents a less daunting prospect than one filled with unrelieved masses of black type.
- Use bullet points or numbered lists rather than cramming a lot of items into densely-worded sentences or paragraphs.
- To ensure consistency, it is a good idea to keep a 'style list' of issues that affect your layout, for example, how your headings and subheadings are organized and presented, how you list items and how you cross-refer to other parts of the report.
- The overall look of the report should be simple and clear, with plenty of white space on the page. Even if this makes it longer, it will be easier to read (and easier to write) and will create a better impression.

Paper

There are various types and qualities of paper available to be used in printing your report. The most common way of grading paper is in terms of its weight, measured in grams per square metre (gsm). The higher the gsm, the stronger the paper will be, and this may be a factor you will have to consider, especially if you decide to have your report printed, book-style, on both sides of each sheet. The standard weight of decent-quality paper is 80gsm, rising to 80–100gsm for high-quality varieties. You will probably not need to go as high as 130gsm, which is mainly used for prestige stationery. Here is a rough guide to paper qualities:

- **all-purpose paper.** As the name suggests, this will supply a good printing result for most needs, and is especially recommended if you want your report to look important.
- **laser paper.** More expensive than standard paper, this will give the best results when used in a laser printer, especially when using more than one colour of ink.
- **inkjet paper.** Less expensive than all-purpose or laser paper, this will give perfectly good results in inkjet printers but is not recommended for laser printers
- **copy paper.** This is the all-purpose paper for office use. It is designed to achieve high-quality photocopies but will perform well in basic printing (not colour).
- **economy paper.** This is the cheapest type of paper, suitable for everyday printing and copying. It is not recommended for an important report.

The colour of paper to be used is also a consideration. White is of course the standard everyday colour, with off-white or cream often chosen for a more prestigious look, just as with stationery for correspondence. It really is a matter of choice, though, and blue, pink, green or yellow may strike you as eye-catching. Providing the ink colour is appropriate, there is no reason why your report should not be printed perfectly legibly on a colour of paper that appeals to you. Think about the readers, however, and try to tailor this to what you think will impress or appeal to them.

Binding

If your report is only a couple of pages long, this section will not concern you. Binding considerations will only come into play for longer documents. Once again, there are various options open to you and your choice may depend on budget or on how impressive you want your report to be. Here is a list of the most common type of binding that we are going to look at in detail:

- ring binding
- comb binding
- coil binding
- thermal binding
- saddle stitching
- side stitching
- perfect binding
- case binding
- lamination

Ring binding

Most people will be familiar with ring binders: the type of loose-leaf binder that has two or more metal rings along the inside spine, which opens to hold perforated sheets of paper. The chief advantage of this type of binder is the ease of removing or inserting pages. The cover can be stiff or flexible, sometimes with a transparent sheath that allows you to insert a cover page. Alternatively, you may be able to have the title of your report printed on the front cover.

Comb binding

The 'comb' referred to here is a length of plastic used to form the spine of the document. It grips the paper by means of projections (like particularly thick teeth on a comb) that slot through rectangular holes punched in each sheet. This relatively inexpensive method has the advantage of allowing your report to lie flat on a desk when it is opened.

Coil binding

This is the type of binding often used for calendars, manuals and notebooks. In this method the sheets are held together at the spine by a single coil of metal or plastic wire that passes through the many perforations at the back of each page. This is more expensive than comb binding, but it gives a professional finish, with different colours of coil available. Like comb binding, coil binding allows the document to be opened out flat.

Thermal binding

In this method, heat is used to melt adhesive strips placed along the spine of the document. This does away with the need for punching or perforation of the pages, as in the techniques described above, and makes a firm binding.

Saddle stitching or stapling

This technique is often used for magazines or booklets and involves assembling a number of folded sheets, one within the next, and stitching them together through the centre of their folds. If staples rather than stitches are used, it is called saddle stapling.

Side stitching or stapling

This method is sometimes used when the page size is too large to allow saddle stitching. In this case the pages are stitched or stapled on the side of the sheet, a little way in from the spine. One drawback with this method is that the document can't be opened out flat.

Perfect binding

Paperback books are the most common use for this method of binding, but telephone directories and magazines can also be bound in this way. The pages are held together, an adhesive is applied to the spine and a limp cover is put on, to be held by the same glue that holds the pages together. Obviously, this type of binding is only applicable when your report has a substantial number of pages, but if used it will give the document the professional appearance of a paperback book.

Case binding

You will really only come across this type of binding on hardback books. The pages are sewn or glued together at the spine and a cloth strip is attached down its length. A cardboard cover (known as a case) is then glued on. This is an expensive form of binding, but if your report is large and important enough to merit it, this type of binding is sturdy, enduring and very impressive.

Lamination

This is a form of protection for a document or its cover in which a thin transparent sheet of plastic is applied to form a permanent coating. You will see this on such printed matter as restaurant menus, recipe books and manuals; basically on material that is expected to be semi-permanent and undergo a lot of handling. Lamination might be an attractive option, not for the pages but for the cover of your report.

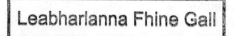

Index

N

notes (in report) **50–2**, 56–7
noun **70–1**
numbering
of diagrams **51–2**, 153–4
of notes 50–1
of points 11, **48–50**, 117
number of words 17
numbers (in text) **110–15**

O

offensive language. *See* sensitive
language

P

paper **170–1**
paragraphs **69**, 169
length **63–4**, 131
parts of speech **69–77**
period. *See* full stop
pie charts **155**, 162–3
place names 108–9
plain English **131**
See also vocabulary
plan **19–21**, 34, 36, 63
plurals
forming 88, **93–5**
of abbreviations 110
political correctness 137, 143
predictive spelling 92
preposition **75–6**
presentation **164–74**
binding **171–4**
layout **170**
paper **170–1**
typography
procedure **46–7**
progress report **13**
pronoun **74–5**

proofreading **160–4**
proper names 101–2, **106–9**
proper noun **70**, 101–2, 107
punctuation **78–90**

Q

quality monitoring report **13–14**
question mark **80**
questionnaire **23–4**
quotation marks **85–6**
double or single 85
to enclose quotations 105–6
to enclose speech 104–5
to indicate titles 86, 107
to indicate translation of foreign
title 119
to indicate unusual use of word
121–2
quotations **105–6**
quotes. *See* quotation marks

R

recommendations **54–5**
reference books 24
references 56, **57–8**
register 152
regular verb 71
repetitiveness. *See* waffle
research **22–31**
Internet, the 25–6
interviews and meetings 22–3
libraries 24–5
reading 29–31
surveys and questionnaires 23–4
research report **14**

S

semicolon **83**
in lists 116
sensitive language **137–44**